A Jewel in His Crown by Priscilla Evans Shirer is challenging, inspiring, encouraging and heartwarming. Her message will give the man of God a deeper love and appreciation for a woman of God. It's a beautiful book.

Zig Ziglar
Author/Motivational Teacher

Priscilla Evans Shirer has taken scriptural truth and translated it into such practical application there will be no excuse for not grasping the valuable insights she shares. Still she goes one step further by being vulnerable and transparent. As she shares her own personal struggles and victories, Priscilla becomes a writer you can touch as well as learn from.

Michelle McKinney Hammond
Author of *What to Do Until Love Finds You*
and *Secrets of an Irresistible Woman*

Priscilla is a Jewel in the Crown of all who meet her. She bubbles over with enthusiasm and lights up every room she enters. I know this book will be a blessing to all who read it and will reserve each woman a place in the King's court.

Florence Littauer
Author and Speaker
Silver Boxes, Personality Plus,
Getting Along with Almost Anybody

Priscilla Evans Shirer communicates with an authority and wisdom well beyond her years. She understands her value in Christ and His purpose for her life, and the resulting confidence and enthusiasm are highly contagious.

Twila Paris
Contemporary Christian
Recording Artist

REDISCOVERING
YOUR VALUE AS
A WOMAN
OF EXCELLENCE

A
JEWEL
IN HIS
CROWN

Priscilla Evans Shirer

MOODY PRESS
CHICAGO

Moody Press, a ministry of Moody Bible Institute,
is designed for education, evangelization, and edification.
If we may assist you in knowing more about Christ
and the Christian life, please write us without obligation:
Moody Press, c/o MLM, Chicago, Illinois 60610.

All Scripture quotations, unless indicated, are taken from the *New American Standard Bible* © 1960, 1963, 1968, 1971, 1972, 1973, 1975, 1977, and 1994 by the Lockman Foundation, and are used by permission.

Scripture quotations marked (NIV) are taken from the *Holy Bible: New International Version*®. NIV®. Copyright © 1973, 1978, 1984 by International Bible Society. Used by permission of Zondervan Publishing House. All rights reserved.

The "NIV" and "New International Version" trademarks are registered in the United States Patent and Trademark Office by International Bible Society. Use of either trademark requires permission of International Bible Society.

Scripture quotations marked(KJV) are taken from the King James Version.

ISBN: 0-8024-4097-5

3 5 7 9 10 8 6 4 2

Printed in the United States of America

This book is lovingly dedicated to my mother.
You are the true picture of grace, elegance, and dignity. I am grateful
that God decided to give me to you. It is in you that I have seen my true
model of the woman of excellence.

CONTENTS

FOREWORD

I have come to know Priscilla Evans Shirer, both personally and professionally.

Hers is a fresh, unspoiled voice—in song and in writing. Priscilla is one of those people who tells the truth, who gives her audiences and her readers a true picture of what it means to be a godly woman—not just when the spotlight is on, but in everyday life. She is confident and assertive, a woman of a multitude of talents and gifts—not the least of which is communicating God's truth with power and effectiveness.

The issue of character as a Christian woman is at the forefront of Priscilla's passion and vision. She knows how important it is that each woman has a clear knowledge of who she is, whose she is, and where she is going. And that's what *A Jewel in His Crown* is all about. In these pages Priscilla reveals to all God's women who they are in Christ—Daughters of King Jesus—and what He has in store for those who follow Him. She shows how God can redeem them from the pain of their sin and exchange it all for a new joy that can't even begin to be fully understood this side of heaven.

She rightly recognizes that God's Word has something to say about every decision in life, and she offers practical advice on finding out God's special purposes and design for each woman He has created.

Priscilla has spoken the message of this book to live audiences all across the country, with life-changing results. Now in written form, this will be an even more powerful tool for women who are not ashamed to be labeled as "followers of God."

God richly bless you as you read and apply these practical truths from His Word.

And may you always walk the walk.

KIRK FRANKLIN

Especially for…

Daddy, I love you so much. My aspiration in life is to be like you when I grow up! You are a true minister of what the power of God can do in the lives of those who obey. You have taught me the importance of integrity and character because who you are in the light, you are in the dark. Thank you for your character. I am privileged to be your little girl. For all of your diligence, time, and attention in reminding me of my worth in Christ, I am truly grateful. I hope my children will someday see in me what I see in you: a friend, a teacher, a confidant, and an encourager.

Aaron and Malita, Eric and Yvette, Ikki and Tara, you will never know how much your encouragement, prayers, and support helped me during one of the roughest times of my life. You are certainly true friends indeed. Thank you for reminding me that I am "a jewel in His crown."

My sister Chrystal, and my brothers Anthony and Jonathon, I can't imagine life without you. We have shared everything, and you have helped to shape my life. I look up to you for your courage, admire you for your diligence, and aspire to attain to your standards of excellence. Thank you for giving me the gift of best friends.

Sharon and Jada, thank you for keeping me accountable and guiding me through many twists and turns in my short life.

Auntie, I love you and appreciate you. For all the days and nights that you spent praying, fasting, and talking and listening to me, I am truly grateful. Your life is a ministry to me, and my prayer is that I am blessed to be half of the aunt that you have been.

To my sweet niece Kariss. You are the apple of my eye. When you were born, I was the first person to touch you. When I felt your warm touch, I prayed right there in the delivery room that the Lord would keep you in His perfect care and protection. Since that time, I have prayed constantly for you that as you find your way in this life you will lay aside any sin and hindrance that will so easily entangle you and will run with endurance the race set before you. You are a beautiful girl, and God has blessed you in immeasurable ways already. Never forget that you are "a jewel in His crown."

And finally, to Jerry, the Lord sent you into my life when I least expected it, but most needed it. You came and gave back to me that which was once lost. Thank you for being my restorer, my shade, my covering, my sanctifier, my savior, my satisfier, my friend, and my husband (and I could go on). You are my miracle, and I will spend my lifetime dedicated to loving you more and more. Thank you for reminding me everyday that I am special in your eyes.

Chapter One

DIAMONDS IN THE KING'S CROWN

*H*ave you ever stopped to admire the dazzling gems displayed in a fine jewelry store? Spotlights ignite beautiful sapphires, rubies, emeralds, and diamonds, setting them ablaze with color. Gold gleams, silver shines, and a glittering array of gemstones captivates us with its fire. It's difficult to walk by a jeweler's window without taking a moment or two to look a little closer.

A jewel is an exquisite object, sparkling with light, something that is prized and treasured. It is looked upon with awe and wonder. Those who see it partake in its beauty, finding themselves delighted simply by having been in its presence. Usually when we have the opportunity to see a fine jewel on display, we feel a longing to possess it, wishing we had the money to buy it. Most of us can only dream of obtaining something of such fine quality. It is far too expensive for us.

More exquisite than any other is the rare jewel we call a diamond. A diamond is not easily attainable, and its value far exceeds the worth of regular jewelry. Women everywhere dream of the day when a man who loves them will buy a beautiful diamond ring to symbolize the rare eternal love that exists between them. For most women, a ruby or sapphire will not do. Although they are both beautiful stones, they are not worth as much. A diamond is more precious because it is uncommon and nearly indestructible. A diamond does not declare its value in a flashy or obnoxious way; only subtly does it reveal its quiet beauty.

The lucky person who has the opportunity to own such a treasure will certainly handle it with care. Diamonds are often kept in security boxes, not brought out except on a few occasions—very special occasions. A diamond is protected and cared for with great diligence. Why? Because it is not only a jewel of great beauty; it is also rare.

Webster's dictionary describes a jewel as "a precious stone or any person or thing that is very dear to one." The dictionary goes on to describe the term *rare* as "not frequently found; scarce or uncommon; unusually good or excellent." By putting those two definitions together we can infer that rare jewels are things or people who are precious because they are good, excellent, and not frequently found.

JEWELS FOR THE KING'S CROWN

In our lives the Lord blesses us by placing different people in different seasons to give us what we need at those particular times. He uses their weaknesses and strengths to remind us of what He expects of us. There are some women who I have encountered who exemplify women of dignity and distinction—they are rare jewels. I have learned from them by observing them, and I hope that you, too, can learn from them and their struggles.

You've probably heard of Elisabeth Elliot. She is a woman of God if ever I have known one. I've never had the privilege of meeting her, yet I feel as if I know her. I have faithfully listened to her radio broadcasts. I have read every book she has authored that I could get my hands on. My name is on her mailing list, and I want to hear everything she has to say. Why? Because I'm convinced that Elisabeth Elliot is a woman of distinction.

In her writings she will tell you that she has never considered herself to be a beautiful woman. She sees herself as an average person. However, she does not let this deter her from presenting herself as a woman of the King's court. She has followed the Lord and lived for Him in every way that she can. She was and remains a quiet woman who is disciplined in her service to Jesus Christ. Elisabeth ministers to thousands of people all over the world. They are touched by the godly confidence she has in herself, and she teaches others to gain the same confidence.

Most people know of her because of her wisdom regarding dating and relationships. She is an expert not because of academic studies, but because of what she has been through: Elisabeth Elliot has had her heart broken.

Years ago Elisabeth met a man named Jim Elliot, and the two fell in love with each other. For five years, they waited on God to bring them together. This entire time they remained pure and holy before the Lord.

Elisabeth esteemed herself highly enough to wait for the appointed time for her union to the man who she believed was the one for her. She did not chase him, even when he seemed disinterested or when she felt impatient. She waited on God to move. At last they were married, and only a year and a half later he was killed—martyred in South America while doing Christian missionary work.

What immense pain and anguish Elisabeth must have felt after the loss of the only man she'd ever loved. But still she served God wholly and loved Him all the more because of His goodness. Much more than that has taken place in the life of Elisabeth Elliot—she has been through both good things and bad things. The way she has handled both the triumphs and the heartaches of her life speaks of her high view of her position in Christ Jesus. She is a woman of excellence whose life's goal is to adorn the crown of her Master. Elisabeth Elliot is a diamond in the King's crown.

About a year ago I had the privilege of meeting Anne Graham Lotz. She amazed me with her sense of dignity and pride as God's woman. Anne Graham Lotz is the daughter of Billy Graham. She is a speaker who boldly proclaims the good news of Jesus Christ.

Before I was introduced to her at a conference in Atlanta, I had heard about her and was delighted to finally meet her. I immediately recognized an air about her that made me want to get to know her better. I automatically wondered what made this woman tick. What was the force behind her power? She is stunningly beautiful on the outside, but that has absolutely nothing to do with the amazing presence that she has.

My mother had told me that a group of friends were sitting down to eat dinner one evening and Anne was asked to pray over the meal. My mom couldn't help but open her eyes and watch her as Anne talked to the Lord. The tone in her voice and the power that filled the room through her words were awesome. To hear Anne Graham Lotz speak is an experience, but to hear her pray is amazing!

When I met Anne Graham Lotz, one particular experience cemented my opinion that surely she recognized her position as a woman in the King's court. At one point during the conference, she walked right up to me and smiled sweetly. She took my hand and said some words that I will never forget:

"Priscilla, both of our fathers are famous guys who have a huge following. People always want to know and hear what they have to say. But I want to encourage you to do what the Lord has called you to do and not worry about how big your father's ministry is. God has not called you or me to do what our fathers are doing. He has called us to do something different."

We were standing in the foyer of a very prestigious hotel. There were big-name authors, musical artists, and preachers everywhere. Anne looked around and said, "Priscilla, half of these people with these big ministries are going to get to heaven and find out that they weren't even on the front lines. I just want to be on the front lines. I want to get to heaven and find out that God was pleased with what I did for Him here."

How powerful those words were to me! Anne was not concerned with what other people thought of her or her ministry. She wanted what the Father wanted for her, and nothing more. She wanted to share Jesus with as many people as possible. She was not concerned if her ministry was not as big and recognizable as her earthly father's; she was concerned only with pleasing her heavenly Father. She is a woman whose eyes are fixed not on the things of this world but on the things of the Lord.

Anne Graham Lotz is a diamond in the King's court, an adornment on His crown.

Mary, the mother of Jesus, was a woman of excellence. She not only gave birth to our Lord and Savior, but she was the one who reared Him and loved Him so that He might love the world. In a day and time when pregnancy outside of marriage was punishable by death, this woman trusted God with her circumstances. She believed that God had spoken to her and that He knew just how to take care of her despite the problems that she might face because of her situation.

Mary had just become engaged to Joseph when an angel spoke to her and told her what was in store for her life. How afraid she must have been! Not only was she going to have a baby, supernaturally fathered by the Holy Spirit, but she also had to tell the man to whom she was betrothed that she was pregnant, and that the baby was not his. I imagine Mary was very worried that Joseph would reject her and refuse to be with her.

How ludicrous her story must have sounded! Can you imagine telling your boyfriend that, yes, you're pregnant with somebody else's baby, but an angel has appeared to you and told you that the child you're carrying will save the world from its sins? Joseph would surely think that she had lost her mind. Worse yet, he had the legal right to cause Mary to be stoned to death on charges of promiscuity.

Yet despite all of these fears, Mary trusted God and believed that He was going to take care of her. She had faith in Him and His plan. She relied on His promises, even when the circumstances said that she was in big trouble.

How godly and upright Mary must have been to be chosen as the mother of our Lord. God looked down on the earth and saw many women who were potential mothers for Jesus, but after the search was complete, He chose Mary. She was a virtuous woman who loved and cherished both herself and her Lord enough to go through what was undoubtedly the most agonizing experience of her life. No matter what the cost, she counted it all joy to suffer for the sake of her Lord. This woman, the mother of Jesus, was a diamond in the King's court. Today she still shines as an adornment on His crown.

Elizabeth Cannings is also a woman of excellence. She is my mother's sister, and my father describes her as the godliest woman that he knows. She is a beautiful woman who desires only to serve Christ. She has all of the qualities of the virtuous Proverbs 31 woman. She is a hard worker and is known for diligence in her service.

Elizabeth has been involved in ministry of some form or fashion for many years. She works without complaining or grumbling because she knows that her reward comes from the highest Source. She was very instrumental in raising us four Evans kids, and we all call her "Auntie."

To me, Auntie has always been a powerful example of the way a woman should be and act. She holds the Bible in high esteem and lives her life according to its precepts. She has had many suitors but has remained single and a virgin all her life. Her standards are very high because she is a rare jewel. At forty-three years of age, she doesn't allow men in her home unless others are there. This is a rule most people my age don't think to follow.

My aunt Elizabeth wants to make sure that she glorifies God with her body as well as her mind and spirit. She is never in the limelight; she just quietly does her work with a smile. She is loving and caring and very dependable. She is godly and the world knows it, not because she tells everyone with her words, but because she tells everyone with her life. This is one woman whom I would love to pattern myself after. Elizabeth Cannings adorns the King's crown as a diamond in His court.

Hannah, the mother of the Old Testament prophet Samuel, was a woman of excellence. She prayed for years that the Lord would give her a son. She was heartsick because she couldn't get pregnant. But she did not let this ruin her relationship with her Lord. She kept her eyes focused on Him and on what she believed He could do for her.

In the ancient world where she lived, when a woman could not conceive, she was looked upon with contempt and scorn. She was considered worthless to her husband, her family, and her community. Because of her plight, Hannah could have become embittered toward God. There she was, serving and loving Him as she should be, and the one thing that would make her acceptable in the sight of others, He would not grant to her. Yet even though Hannah was discouraged about her inability to conceive, she kept her eyes focused on God and His righteousness.

Hannah probably felt both worthless and powerless. She knew that she was disgraced in the eyes of the people. She knew that when others looked at her, they were dissatisfied with the outcome of her life. She felt like she had little value. However, she believed that God had a plan that was bigger than either her longings or her timetable. She somehow managed to cling to the confidence that God was working to do something even greater than fulfilling her desire for a child. She knew that her heavenly Father could and would accomplish something wonderful in her life if she would just trust Him and wait on Him.

Hannah recognized that her God was able to do exceeding abundantly beyond all that she could ask or think (Ephesians 3:20). God strongly supports women who rest in Him and are willing to wait on Him to complete things in their lives. He is pleased when women believe that He knows what He is doing and are willing to submit themselves to His timing.

Have you ever felt worthless? I know I have at times. Maybe your friends and family have been disheartened by the fact that you never finished high school or college. Perhaps you have not achieved what they thought you should have. Possibly you just don't quite measure up to their standards. If that describes your situation, you can be sure of one thing: God has a mighty plan for you just as He did for Hannah. And right now, this very minute, God is working all things together for your good (Romans 8:28).

If Hannah had been outside of the will of God, she would not have experienced all the joy and blessing that God intended for her. If she had given birth to Samuel any earlier than at the intended time, it would have been the wrong time. God had a plan that exceeded Hannah's deepest desire. He was interested in what her son would do for the entire nation of Israel.

What does God want to do for you? If you will wait to receive it, your blessings will be tenfold. If God does it according to your timetable, you might just miss out on the entire blessing that He has for you. Women of excellence must remember that God has far bigger, far better plans than ours.

Hannah is a woman in the King's court; she is a diamond who adorns His crown.

Terry Willits is a woman of excellence. She is an author and speaker who uses her skills as an interior decorator to teach women how they can best make their homes glorifying to God. Her quiet yet bubbly personality has changed the lives of many women who want to make their homes places where their families can find rest.

Terry and her husband have been married for twelve years and would love to have children, but God seems to have other plans. Terry, like a modern-day Hannah, has trusted the Lord for her children and has asked the Lord, "Well, if not children, then what?" She doesn't complain and cause a commotion. She just rests and trusts that God has another plan.

Terry's willingness to simply rely on Jesus has touched me deeply. I am humbled by this woman who is tiny in stature yet huge in faith. Terry knows that the Lord has birthed a ministry through her that has helped women everywhere. She is an awesome example of how women of the kingdom should make sure that their homes come first. She has made her husband and her home her first priority, and even though she travels extensively, she still focuses on home and the beauty and rest that her family is able to find there.

Terry Willits is a diamond in the King's court, beautifully adorning His crown.

Martha was a woman of excellence, even though many people continue to give her a hard time. When Jesus visited their home, the two sisters, Mary and Martha, greeted Him and served Him. Mary was the one who took time to sit at His feet and bask in His presence. Martha was the one who was in the kitchen preparing for Him, trying to serve Him well and make everything perfect.

Although Mary's position at Jesus' feet was very important, so was Martha's position in the kitchen. As she hurried around to prepare things, she asked the Master why Mary wasn't helping her. She felt as if she were doing everything on her own. She was tired and frustrated because she was wiping herself out for Jesus.

Martha sets an amazing example for all of us who seek to serve the Lord. Of course we must not allow our service, labor, and responsibilities to distract us from our intimate relationship with Christ. We must keep our priorities in order. But what is more beautiful than a woman who diligently serves and waits on the Master? She doesn't serve Him leftovers. She gives Him only the best. Martha's desire was to make sure that Jesus was well taken care of. Her service was excellent.

I think we can safely say that the only reason that Mary could relax and enjoy the presence of Jesus was because Martha was diligent. If Martha had done her work sloppily, Mary would have had to get up, get busy, and help her. Mary could sit at the feet of Jesus because Martha had swept the floor on which she sat. Although Martha's actions kept her away from positioning herself in front of Jesus, her heart was one of service and diligence. Martha is a diamond in the King's court, adorning the King's crown.

Terry Meeuwsen is a woman of excellence. She is a precious gem who exudes the beauty and femininity of womanhood. I have become fairly well acquainted with this godly woman because I've been a speaker with the Aspiring Women Conference, and Terry is the cohostess of the event.

Terry is a former Miss America and is presently the cohostess of the *700 Club,* along with Pat Robertson. I had watched her on TV for years and had always thought that she is a beautiful woman. But how much more gorgeous she is to me now that I know her. She is warm and caring and loves the Lord with all of her heart.

In my travels I have encountered many women who are well known, and I have been disturbed to find that many of them are so consumed by what they have accomplished that they have forgotten the real reason they've accomplished it. They don't seem to remember that their efforts should be focused on giving God glory, not on glorifying themselves. Terry is a woman who knows whose daughter she is, and she uses her status in life to give her Father glory.

Terry is humble and a pleasure to be around. Some women make you want to know them better and better, and she is one of those women. Her warmth draws you to her. As I sat and talked with her on the first day we met, she asked me whether or not I was married. I said no, but I went on to tell her about some of the guys who were hanging around trying to get my attention. I mentioned one man in particular, whom I was considering marrying.

I will never forget the power and gentleness of Terry's advice as she used Scripture to encourage me to wait on the Lord and trust in Him for guidance. She offered the truth of God with wholehearted sincerity. Terry knows God's Word so well that she is able to minister to anybody anywhere in a gentle and profound way. Her style draws people not only to herself but also to Jesus. I pray that as I grow in the Lord, I will be able to minister to others as Terry Meuwsun ministers to me. She is a diamond in the King's court!

These women are jewels. They are rare jewels, priceless, beautiful and full of light and life. They are examples of godly women who know who they are in Christ Jesus. Their self-esteem is rooted in their relationship to Him, and others are blessed because of it.

While at first glance women like these may seem out of reach to us, they are just like you and me. They have faced issues like dating, singleness, marriage, children, divorce, disease, loneliness, debt, and anxiety. These women have been right where you are.

Satan has attempted at many times to get them to forget their value as daughters of God. However, these women of the King's court have decided never to let him have the upper hand. They have chosen to stand on the authority and promises of God's Word. They possess no more strength than you or I do. They too have faced failure and made mistakes, but they have chosen to remember that the Bible says He "has granted to us everything pertaining to life and godliness" (2 Peter 1:3).

ONE SPECIAL, BRILLIANT GEM

Of all the beautiful gems I have encountered in the King's court, I want to tell you about one who truly is a rare and precious jewel. My mother Lois is a diamond of extremely high quality. Perhaps it is a cliché to refer to our mothers as priceless women, but it is no secret that because my mother realizes her worth as a woman of the King, everyone around her benefits from it.

Just as the beauty of a diamond speaks for itself, my mother doesn't speak often and she never speaks too loudly, but what she does say with her life is inevitably profound. She never announces her entrance in loud clothes, heavy makeup, or a strident voice. But everyone knows when she has entered the room. She smiles sweetly and has a graciousness about her that draws admiration from all. No wonder my father was attracted to her some thirty years ago, and no wonder he is still in love with her today.

When my mother was in her teenage years and early twenties, she was quiet and meek. She looked after her younger brothers and sisters with great affection and pride, and made an early decision that her life would be dedicated to ministry. She was never rambunctious and didn't get into trouble. She listened, learned, and obeyed my grandmother and grandfather.

My mother met my father when she was eighteen years old. At the time, she made it very clear to him that she was the daughter of King Jesus. Because of her position in Christ, there were certain things that she would not do and certain places that she would not go. She didn't believe that she was superior to others, but she knew that she was in a position of royalty that required her to conduct herself in a unique way. My mother has always treasured her role as a woman in the King's court, and she has always taught her children to treasure that position as well.

As women in a royal position, serving a royal God, we must give our very best. My mother has always lived by this standard of excellence. My father often jokes in his sermons that she fell in love with him first, but I truly doubt that. My mother's sweet spirit, high value of herself, and willingness to go where God leads are what attracted my father to my mother. They continue to attract many others to her even now.

When they were newlyweds, my parents had very little to call their own. They lived on three hundred dollars a month, yet my mother still held her head up high because she refused to let her external circumstances determine her worth. In fact, I have often found that women who have had to go through a period of struggle often have a higher estimation of themselves. Sometimes material things strip from us what really matters the most.

My mother is never flamboyant. In fact, she goes out of her way to make sure that she isn't. As a child, I watched my mother trying on the clothes that she planned to wear to one event or another. She would walk in front of the mirror in the hallway to check out her ensemble's taste and modesty. If she would be singing that evening, I can remember seeing her try out the movements that she might make while singing in order to be sure that her skirt would not reveal too much of her body. I find myself doing the same thing as I get older.

As my mother has matured, she has become an excellent wearer of hats. In the African-American culture everybody knows that the first lady of the church is always adorned in the finest hat around—it's a tradition. Well my mother has never been the traditional pastor's wife. She hardly ever wore hats until I was well into my teenage years. But when she does, the hats and outfits that she wears are magnificent. She looks marvelous in them.

My mother has always wanted to look nice in order to represent her status as a daughter of King Jesus. Yet she does not want to draw undue attention to herself and away from her Savior. She has the perfect blend of respect for herself and honor for the house of God. If you are royalty, you don't have to flaunt it—people will just know. They will know because of the air that you carry, not because of the stuff that you carry. My mother is a prime example of a woman in the King's court. A diamond doesn't have to be flashy or flamboyant to be breathtakingly beautiful.

SHINING FROM THE INSIDE OUT

If you're like me, you may find yourself a little discouraged after meeting the women of excellence I've described for you. Maybe their godly attributes and spiritual qualities seem unattainable. The good news is, they're not. The most amazing thing about being women in the King's Court is that all of us—no matter how we see ourselves—are beautiful in His sight. He continues to polish and refine us to make every facet of our personalities a shining reflection of His love. But of course His refining work takes time—often a lifetime.

One day as I was reading Scripture, I came across 1 Peter 3:4, which states that women are to have a gentle and quiet spirit. As soon as I read that, I felt very dismayed because I am neither quiet nor gentle. Quite to the contrary, I am loud and obnoxious and always wanting to be involved. I felt kind of upset. It seemed that in order to be a woman who adorned the Father's crown as a precious jewel, I had to exhibit characteristics that I was certain I did not have.

"It isn't fair," I told the Lord. "You know I can't be quiet. I talk for a living, for goodness' sake! I'm rather brash on occasion and would find it quite hard to be gentle in speech and action."

That was one time in my life that the Lord spoke very clearly to me, almost audibly. He said, "Priscilla, why would I ask you to be something that you don't have the potential to be? In fact, why would I create you in a way that is contrary to My Word?" He wouldn't. I just thought that I couldn't be that way because of the characteristics that I was most accustomed to exhibiting. Those words from the Lord meant just one thing: *change.*

When we come to the cross of Jesus, everything changes—especially our inner selves. Whatever we are accustomed to in our personalities or character, if those qualities don't line up with Scripture, they must cease. Just because some actions are the norm in your life doesn't mean that they are right.

Sometimes it is relatively simple to change ourselves on the outside. We can stop wearing short dresses, and stop drinking, and maybe even stop hanging around with people who don't treat us like royalty. But the issue is deeper than that. God wants to change everything that you thought made up your very existence—everything you thought made you who you are. Is He asking too much? No, He is not. You are a woman in His court and, more importantly, you are His daughter. You are called to "present your body a living and holy sacrifice" to the Lord (Romans 12:1). Maybe we don't feel like it, but offering everything we are to God really is our "reasonable service." Christ has done so much for us. Isn't this the least we can do to thank Him? He wants everything. He wants you and He wants me. He wants to teach us how to know and believe that we are the royal women He has destined us to be. He wants us to recognize the call that He has on our lives and to act accordingly. He doesn't want us to put on a show. He wants us to truly believe in ourselves and our potential *in Him* to achieve great things in His kingdom.

THE POWER TO SHINE

You know it's really not that difficult to look like we are doing all right. How many times have you met someone who made an absolutely wonderful first impression? However once you took a closer look, you found out that there really wasn't much to them.

I once heard Chuck Swindoll tell a story that illustrated this point wonderfully. There was a man who was on a journey one day, and he came to a large body of water. He couldn't walk around it; it was far too big. It looked so intimidating. It was huge, and it made a whole lot of noise as the water ran over the rocks and rushed against the shore. He worried and fretted, but he finally decided that the only way he was going to make it to his destination was if he went straight through the middle.

He took a step in and found that the water close to the shore was only two inches deep. He took a few more steps and realized that it did not get any deeper. He kept walking and soon realized that all the way across the body of water it was only two inches deep. He made it safely to the other side with nothing wet but his shoes.

Unfortunately, that is the way a lot of our lives are. We look really important and we sound really intimidating, but when people take a step into our lives they find that we are only two inches deep! There is nothing to us. We are shallow. There is no quality of character, no depth, and no beauty beyond the surface of our existence. Now, I have to be honest with you—this is one of my greatest fears in life: that I will be more wide than I am deep. My prayer for you and me is that when people take a step into our lives they will find that they are stepping into a deep, clear spring filled with value, glory, and power. I pray that they will find limitless attributes that are waiting to be poured freely out upon the world.

Many things have caused me to look at the issue of self-esteem very seriously. Relationships, friendships, bad decisions and other elements have played a part in my concern. In the chapters that follow, I want to expose self-esteem for what it truly is and explore what it really means in the life of every woman in the King's court.

It dawned on me one day that many people look at me and see the daughter of a famous minister, a well-educated, fairly beautiful, and intelligent woman who has won several pageants, contests, and awards. They immediately assume I have it all together, even though they know little about me beyond those external things. In the same sense, I have seen women who look fabulous and have wonderful husbands and families. They own great cars and lavish houses; they are popular and seem to have everything going for them. I have wondered what could possibly be wrong in their lives. Then it occurred to me: "Wow, I could be just as wrong about them as they could be about me!" Outward appearance is oftentimes a very incorrect indicator of the internal.

It's not difficult to look one way and feel another. In fact, many of the women who look awesome on the outside work very hard to do so with the specific intent of covering up the pain and emptiness they feel on the inside. The truth is, unless you are connected to God—the power source on the inside—you can forget all the work that you are trying to do on the outside. It won't get the job done.

There was a young woman who needed to buy a brand-new refrigerator. She was determined to buy the best one she could find. She wanted the top of the line. So she went to the top-of-the-line store and asked for the top-of-the-line salesman, whom she told to show her the top-of-the-line refrigerator. Well the sales guy showed her a refrigerator for $4,500! Naturally, it was an awesome refrigerator. She purchased it and had it delivered to her home. She went to the grocery store and bought new vegetables, milk, ice cream, and everything else she could think of to put into her new refrigerator. She stocked it and went to bed.

She got up the next morning, and much to her dismay, she found that the ice cream was running down the side of the freezer, the milk was spoiled, and the vegetables had gone bad. The refrigerator was not working. Now she was a Christian, but she was evangelically ticked off! She went to the phone and called the store that had sold her this new refrigerator. When the clerk answered the phone, she proceeded to inform him in no uncertain terms that she had not purchased this brand-new refrigerator only to have all of her food spoil. Her new, top-of-the-line fridge simply did not work.

The sales clerk was mortified and apologized profusely for the mistake. "I am so sorry ma'am. I can't imagine what the problem could be, but before we come out to your house to fix the problem, can I ask you a few questions over the phone?"

The woman was very upset, but she rather haughtily agreed to answer the questions.

The sales clerk said, "Ma'am, will you go over to the refrigerator, and open the door, and see if the light comes on?"

She laid down the phone and went over to the refrigerator. She opened the door. She went back to the phone and said, "No sir, the light did not come on."

He said, "OK, Ma'am, will you put your head down by the base of the refrigerator and see if you hear a motor running?"

She went over to the refrigerator and leaned down to the bottom.

She went back to the phone. "No, I don't hear the motor running. As I told you, the refrigerator does not work!"

Then the clerk said, "Ma'am just one more thing. Will you please look behind the refrigerator? There is a black cord back there. Will you check to see whether or not it is plugged into the wall?"

She set the phone down and walked to the back of the refrigerator. Wouldn't you know it, lo and behold, she hadn't plugged it in.

The woman walked back to the phone and said, "For $4,500, I shouldn't have to plug it in!"

You may laugh, but unfortunately, that is precisely the way

that many of us live our lives. We spend all kinds of money on our Bally memberships. We invest in our makeup, hair, and nails. We buy classy cars and elegant houses and carry fine leather briefcases to our impressive jobs. But even though we spend all the money in the world on the outside of ourselves, we can never fully cover up the mess on the inside. Sooner or later, somebody is going to find out that we aren't what we claim to be.

We can't shine on the outside unless God's power is at work on the inside. No matter how much work we put into the outside, it will be worthless unless we are plugged into the true power source of our beauty. All the makeup in the world will not matter when the inside is a mess.

DIAMONDS IN THE ROUGH

Have you ever thought of yourself as a diamond in the rough? That's how God sees us all—even the beautiful women we talked about earlier. He is always at work in our lives, helping us shine brighter and more radiantly for Him. I want to explore with you the inside of ourselves. I want to help you discover whatever may be hindering you from reaching your true potential as a beautiful, rare jewel in the King's court. Let's take a long, clear look at ourselves today and ask the Lord to show us what He'd like to do in our hearts and lives.

Are you prepared to allow God's power to transform you from within? That's what this book is about. Isn't it time for you to stop blaming everybody else for your failures, for your seeming inability to excel at anything? Maybe you are reading this book to-day and you are successful and everyone looks at you in awe. You are talented and captivating. Are you using your talents to cover up the mess that needs to be cleaned up on the inside? Are you ashamed of what someone might discover if they took a step into your life and saw the real you? Is there a storm inside that needs the Master's soothing voice to say, "Peace; be still"? Let's look in-side and be honest with ourselves about what we find there.

What keeps us captive to disappointment, disillusionment, and despair? All we need to be women of the kingdom we already have in our possession. All of those external things that can be wrong in life—negative relationships, bad habits, dishonesty, debts, fear, and anger—are reflections of a much deeper issue. It is time for us to see ourselves as God Almighty sees us. Time to stop allowing others to dictate our value and worth. Time for us to take off the masks that disguise the truth about ourselves and to get real with God.

He knows all about our hurt and our pain. He knows that we struggle when we have to wait on Him and rely on Him. He also knows that it is during our times of struggling and waiting and wondering that we develop character that will last for a lifetime. There is a big plan at work that we can't see right now. According to Romans 8:28, God is working everything together for our good. Can you believe that?

My desire is that we will strive to be women of excellence, following the example of women like those I've introduced to you. Let's lay everything aside that could possibly steal our self-esteem from us and remember that God has created us with inestimable value. Naturally, Satan wants us to forget who we really are. He knows that we will fall for anything if we fail to see ourselves as God sees us. He knows that we'll go places we're not supposed to go and that we'll do things we're not supposed to with people we're not supposed to hang out with—all in an attempt to seize what God has already promised us in His Word. Satan knows that the key to our success or failure in this life is found in our self-esteem. That's why it's so important for us to acknowledge today that we are women of the King's court.

The effect that the information in this book will have on your life is entirely up to you. Pray right now that the Lord will help you to drop the walls of protection that you have built up. Ask him to help you get real about the trash in your life and to come clean with Him. It is time! Today is the day for change and for the renewal of power in our lives. We are about to embark on a journey that will open us up to truth. I am determined to take back what the devil has stolen from me and to reclaim my position as God's rare and precious jewel.

How about you?

Consider This

What does the Lord want to teach you about being a woman of God?

What things have you done that have steered you away from being a woman of excellence?

How do you see yourself?

How do you think others see you?

Are you the woman who is profiled in 1 Peter 3:1–5 or in Proverbs 31? Why or why not?

As a diamond in the rough, what things can you see in yourself that Christ needs to refine?

How do you hope to begin to see yourself differently after you read this book?

Prayer of Dedication

Dear Lord, I, _____,
am tired of feeling negatively about myself. For some reason
I have been discouraged and have not lived in a way that tells
the world of my royal status in Your kingdom. I admit that I am
not perfect and that I need help in these areas:

_____

_____

_____

I pray that You will help me begin to develop into the woman
that You have always meant for me to be. I am making a new
commitment to You today, Lord. I don't want the devil to have
the victory in my life in these areas ever again. I want to always
feel as though I am Your woman and that I am in the center of
Your will for my life. As I read this book, please show me those
things that I need to work on most and give me the right spirit
to make the effort to make changes for the better. My goal is to
live for You. I love You, Lord.

In Jesus' name,
Amen

_____

Today's Date

Chapter Two

ADVANCED TO ROYALTY

$\mathcal{I}$'m so glad that you have decided to embark on this journey of self-discovery with me. By continuing to read and reflect, you are doing something that many women never do—you are taking the initiative to discover the things about yourself that need to change. I'm glad you've found the courage to realize one very important point: *no one can do for you what you must do for yourself.*

Unfortunately, many of us allow the way we feel—esteemed or inferior—to depend upon what others think. We are always interested in how people are going to respond to what we wear and how we look. We wonder whether or not we are "in style" at the moment. We hope our outward appearance sends just the right message about who we are and what we're all about. Advertisers are aware of this trait, and the result is a media feeding frenzy.

Creators of TV commercials and print ads want to convince women like you and me that if we buy what they are selling, we will be the life of the party, make a lot of money, or have the best man in town. If they succeed in convincing us, they know they'll have us wrapped around their little fingers. Sure enough, we sometimes find ourselves buying their products in an effort to gain acceptance from others. Although this tendency is not always a destructive one, generally it means that we may have to compromise what *we* really want for what *somebody else* wants us to have.

Spending too much on products that enhance our self-esteem can be a costly enterprise. It can even become addictive. But there is a worse danger—caring too much about other people's opinions of us can actually be self-destructive.

ONE WOMAN'S STORY

While I was speaking at a recent conference, I had the opportunity to meet a young woman named Allison. Although a lot of women wanted to get in touch with me after the event, only a few actually did so. Not long after the conference was over, I got a call from Allison. She had seemed so vibrant, intelligent, and beautiful when we'd met, giving the impression that she was sitting on top of the world. But when I talked to her on the phone a couple of weeks later, I learned that she was very unhappy. There wasn't much about herself that Allison liked.

Years before, Allison had become an unwed mother and had given up her young child for adoption. That memory haunted her. More recently, her husband, whom she loved dearly, had turned to drugs and alcohol and had asked for a divorce. All the stress in her life had increased her appetite, and she had gained more than twenty pounds. The rejection from her husband and the extra weight she'd gained had aggravated Allison's already injured view of herself. Now she believed that she looked horrible, and she reinforced that belief every time she looked in the mirror.

To make matters worse, Allison had enrolled in beauty school. That could have been a good thing, except that every day she was learning how to make other women look beautiful, and the more she learned the less attractive she felt. All day long she was swamped with new information about hair, makeup, and nails, and she was surrounded by attractive women who were consumed with the idea of being beautiful.

Allison was often sad, and she was rapidly becoming emotionally unable to function well in everyday life. Her poor image of herself led her into serious depression, and she even began to entertain suicidal thoughts. This downward emotional spiral in Allison's life was largely based on her poor self-esteem, and her poor self-esteem was largely based on what she assumed other people thought about her.

Like Allison, some women become so overtaken by the idea that they are insignificant and inferior that they no longer see any reason to live. They even go so far as to take their lives. Most of us don't react so intensely, but even if we don't carry our doubts to that extreme, we still may allow what others say and think to dominate us. Thankfully, as Christian women, we are learning to base our self-image on how God sees us and what He thinks of us. As the King's daughters, we really have only one significant question to answer on the subject: *Who are we in the eyes and mind of our Lord?*

I recently went with my sister and mother to see the movie *Elizabeth*. It was a brilliant portrayal of the reign of Queen Elizabeth I. I particularly recall a line that was said at the very beginning of the film. Elizabeth was hated by her sister Mary, who was the current queen of England. Mary wanted to do everything in her power to keep Elizabeth from reigning as queen, even going to the extent of having her arrested.

When the guards came to take her away, Elizabeth was bewildered and feared for her very life. She knew that her sister hated her and did not want her to reign. However, she did have some encouragement from a friend who was with her when the guards arrived. Her friend looked her in the eyes just before the guards hauled her away and said, "Remember who you are."

This man wanted Elizabeth to remember that no matter what her enemies did or said to her, nothing could negate her rightful position. She was a princess. She was reminded by his statement to hold her head up high. She was royalty.

I want to encourage you to do as Queen Elizabeth did—hold up your head and don't forget the way God sees you. It doesn't matter what circumstances you are up against. Nothing and no one should cause you to drop your eyes to the floor in defeat, for

He is "the One who lifts [your] head" (Psalm 3:3). You are royalty because of your birthright in Christ. No matter what anybody else thinks, you are part of the King's royal court. *Remember who you are!*

PERFECTED BY HIS SPLENDOR

You are the daughter of the most high King, and that makes you a princess! You have royal blood running through your veins. Hold your head up high and know your status. Don't let others determine your position. You have been advanced to royalty! Do you believe that?

Maybe so, but amazingly enough you and I often allow Satan to get the best of us and to fill our minds with things that are untrue about our standing with Christ. We start listening to the wrong messages and being affected by the wrong influences. It is at these times that we tend to stray from the Lord and from His will for us.

You see, if you were a literal princess and you ruled over a nation there would be certain rules that you would follow. You wouldn't just go out and mingle with anybody and everybody you governed. Why? Because when you're in a position of royalty, you don't hang around with bumpkins and peasants.

Suppose you're an earthly princess. You are always aware that there are certain clothes that are appropriate for you to wear and certain foods that are healthy and good for you. You won't use certain words or commit certain acts with certain people for one simple reason: *you are the princess.* It is not that you're better than other people. It's just that you've been called to a different way of acting, living, and being because of your position and status.

As a princess, you would act in a certain way that would be indicative of your royal position. You would be proud of who you are and you would want to guard your sphere of influence. There would be a certain amount of respect that you would demand simply because of your role. How high you would hold your head if you were royalty!

Now stop and think: how much higher should you hold your head right here, right now? *You are royalty because your Father is the*

King of the universe! Your Father rules everything, everybody, everywhere. This doesn't mean that you are better than everybody else is; it does mean that you have been placed in a position that demands respect from others. Shouldn't that keep you from forgetting just how precious and magnificent your position is?

Status is an important thing. How often have you envied someone who has status in the world's eyes? We do it every time we go to the movies and see a movie star whose body or face or manner we wish we could emulate. Sometimes people who have earthly status trust that their place in the world will do for them what only God can do. Even in biblical days status was recognized. Tax collectors were looked upon with disdain and prejudice. Those who carried religious prestige were revered and admired. For different reasons people were either placed on a pedestal or dismissed as unimportant.

However, in Old Testament times, after the great Flood destroyed all the ungodly people of the world, people revered God's men and women. That is certainly not the case today. But in biblical times when a man or woman of God spoke, everybody listened. The reasoning for this was simple. A distinctive form of respect was automatically given to those who belonged to God. The people knew that those who had been called by God to perform His tasks were blessed immeasurably and deserved honor. They were highly regarded simply because of their relationship with God. This didn't mean that the people always followed the prophets words though.

In the book of Joshua, chapter five, the story is told of Joshua preparing for a major battle. He saw a very intimidating man approaching. Joshua looked at the infantry that he had readied for the war and looked at this gallant soldier whom he did not know, and he became afraid. This man was awe-inspiring. Joshua approached him and said, "Whose side are you on?" Basically he was saying, "Look, if you are on our side then we have got this thing together, but if you are on the other side then I'm going home!"

The man looked at Joshua and spoke with pride. He said, "I came as captain of the Lord's army!"

Joshua fell on his face before this man because he respected his status. He didn't come to serve in the ranks; he came to run the whole show. He knew why he was there and didn't allow his focus to be shifted. Whether or not he was liked or disliked was irrelevant. He had a position of royalty because of whom he represented. And believe it or not, so do you and I. This is the way I like to say it—"It ain't about you. It's about who you represent."

CHOSEN BY THE FATHER

God's holy people, the Israelites, always needed to be reminded of their importance in the eyes of God. They had the great privilege of being the men, women, and children that God called His own—His "chosen people." What a privilege to be so loved by God that He would want you and your extended family to stand as his representatives to all men. For a while the Jews cherished their position. Before long, however, they forgot and turned away from God.

We're really no different. When we forget our position in Christ, it is then that we turn away and begin to do our own thing. When we no longer feel as though we have anything to protect, we begin to take our position of royalty for granted, and we do things that are contrary to the will of God.

When we don't cherish a gift, we don't utilize it to its full potential. This is exactly what happened to Jerusalem. The people of Jerusalem turned against God because they forgot how much the Lord loved them and how much He had done for them. After years and years of this disobedience, God spoke to the prophet Ezekiel and told him that his duty was to rebuke Jerusalem for her sin. He was to remind God's people of the status that they had been given. God spoke through Ezekiel to the people:

> As for your birth, on the day you were born your navel cord was not cut, nor were you washed with water for cleansing; you were not rubbed with salt or even wrapped in cloths. No eye looked with pity on you to do any of these things for you, to have compassion on you. Rather you were thrown out into the open field, for you were abhorred on the day you were born. (Ezekiel 16:4–5)

God wanted His people to remember what they were like before He came along. He compared the nation to a baby who had been born and left in a field to die. All alone and naked, this new life was looked upon with disdain and discontent. No one had compassion on this child; instead she was looked upon in total disgust.

Before our encounter with the living, loving, holy God, before we learned to call Him our Father, we were out there all by ourselves. No one loved us enough to save us. Everyone we thought might help us walked away. We were left to die until the Lord stepped in!

> When I passed by you and saw you squirming in your blood, I said to you while you were in your blood, "Live!" I said to you while you were in your blood, "Live!" I made you numerous like plants of the field. Then you grew up, became tall, and reached the age for fine ornaments; your breasts were formed and your hair had grown. Yet you were naked and bare. Then I passed by you and saw you, and behold, you were at the time for love; so I spread My skirt over you and covered your nakedness. I also swore to you and entered into a covenant with you so that you became Mine. (Ezekiel 16:6–8)

The almighty God, King of the universe, saw them and had compassion on them. He loved them when no one else did. He reached down and cleaned up their mess. And that is exactly what God does for us. No matter how big the mess we've made of ourselves, He cleans us up. And then He does more. He clothes us and makes us more numerous and multiplies us and blesses us and enters into a covenant with us that assures us of His love. He cares for us so much that He has chosen us—the women He has saved—to be His precious daughters. He loves us so much that He has entered into a covenant with us that cannot be changed or altered.

God's Word is always true, and He has promised that no matter what others may do, say, or think about us, "I will never leave you nor desert you." (Hebrews 13:5) He loves us enough to resurrect us from the dead remains of our lives, loves us enough to exhort us to "Live!" He isn't finished with Jerusalem or with us:

Then I bathed you with water, washed off your blood from you, and anointed you with oil. I also clothed you with embroidered cloth, and put sandals of porpoise skin on your feet; and I wrapped you with fine linen and covered you with silk. And I adorned you with ornaments, put bracelets on your hands, and a necklace around your neck. I also put a ring in your nostril, earrings in your ears, and a beautiful crown on your head. Thus you were adorned with gold and silver, and your dress was of fine linen, silk, and embroidered cloth. You ate fine flour, honey, and oil; so you were exceedingly beautiful and advanced to royalty. (Ezekiel 16:9–13)

This is truly amazing! God took an unloved orphan and not only gave her a home, a new name, and necessities for survival, but also went way beyond the call of duty and loved this baby. He entered into a covenant with her and advanced her to royalty. Are you aware that the King of Kings and Lord of Lords also did that for you and me? He has clothed us in dignity and hope and righteousness. Do we appreciate what He has done for us enough to live for Him?

Our God, our heavenly Father, has established us as royalty and has invited us to reign with Him. He could have put us in any old kind of clothes. But because we are His daughters, He has dressed us in clothes only suitable for princesses or queens. In biblical days, not everybody wore porpoise-skin sandals, silk, bracelets and embroidered cloth. Only those people who had been established as royal figures could aspire to wear such fine apparel.

Unfortunately, many women don't realize how blessed they are, and they take advantage of what they have been given. They don't appreciate all that God has done for them, so they squander the great inheritance that has been bestowed upon them. That's what Jerusalem did.

Then your fame went forth among the nations on account of your beauty, for it was perfect because of My splendor that I bestowed on you. . . . But you trusted in your beauty and played the harlot because of your fame, and you poured out your harlotries on every passer-by who might be willing. And you took some of your clothes, made for yourself high places of various colors, and played the harlot on them, which should never come about nor happen. You also took your beautiful jewels made of My gold and of My silver, which I had given you, and made for yourself male images that you might play the harlot with them. Then you took your embroidered cloth and covered them, and offered My oil and My incense before them. (Ezekiel 16:14–18)

Jerusalem had forgotten what the Lord had done for her. She no longer considered her great position a gift from the Most High, so she squandered it. How hurt and disappointed God must have been. After all He had done for His people, they continued to act like Gentiles.

They used the riches He had given them to build high places to worship; they exalted man-made images. They forgot that they had been advanced to royalty. They forgot that they had been found, loved, cherished, clothed, anointed, and finally promoted to a position that was unlike any other. They forgot, and they suffered.

Often we worship and praise the creation and forget about the Creator. In fact, that's exactly what we do when we consider others' opinions more important than God's. We know we are idolizing others when we concentrate on them more than we concentrate on God. This, my sister, is sin. One of the Ten Commandments plainly states that we should have no other god before Him. Yet, for all practical purposes, we idolize others and worship their opinions when we allow them to be more significant in our minds and hearts than God is.

God must love us more than we can possibly imagine. He has saved us from the mess we've made of our lives. He has called us to the great privilege of being His daughters of royalty. He is looking forward to developing a never-ending relationship with us as we cherish the gifts that He has given us. Never forget, my sister, that we have been advanced to royalty.

A DECLARATION OF INDEPENDENCE

When a woman recognizes all that she is worth, a new awakening occurs in her. No longer is she held captive by fears, shame, and guilt. She is free to experience the joy of the Lord and to reach the full potential of all that He has in store for her. The Word of God brings liberty. The "truth will set [her] free" (John 8:32)—free to experience the abundance of life that the Father desires for her. Our Father has declared our independence, setting us free so we can walk in delight and dignity with Him.

There are certain Scriptures that the Lord has used to remind me of how important I am to Him. I want to share them with you because it is very important for you to keep them in your heart and mind. These Scriptures should be a constant reminder of your position, your status of royalty.

What better place to begin a journey through the Scriptures than from the very beginning? In the very first book of the Bible, God seems to take a special liking to the female gender. He had created a world full of tremendous things that had never before been created, and whose glory cannot be reproduced ever again. He spent six days taking care of all of the intricate details that would make the earth what it is. He made all sorts of vegetation and all kinds of living creatures. The world God made gave Him great pleasure.

Then He made the most wonderful of all the creatures—the man. So engrossed was our God in this effort that He wanted to breathe into this being His very own breath in order to give him life. On the seventh day of creation, God looked at what He had done and saw that it was good. He rested in the knowledge that what He had made was wonderful and perfect. However, after all of the glorious things that He had accomplished, there was still something missing. There was a lost component, and that missing piece was *woman*.

The woman was the completion of God's greatest creation. Genesis 1:26 says, "Then God said, 'Let Us make man in Our image, according to Our likeness.'" He created man and woman in His own image. Almighty God so esteemed humanity that He actually created you and me in His very own likeness. The Trinity decided that this creation was of such importance, of such dignity, that it should bear the very image of its Creator.

If you are like most women, you have probably looked in the mirror and wondered why in the world God decided to make you the way He did. Maybe you have always been totally dissatisfied with the way you were created, and have always wished for something "better." We are made in God's own likeness; how insulted He must feel when we do this. How dare we insult a holy God, wishing we looked different or were, in fact, different people all together? Wouldn't you be hurt if your son or daughter looked identical to you and hated every minute of it? I wonder how God must feel about us when we cry and pout about the very work of His own hands.

God gave very special attention to the creation of woman. Since this would be the final act of His creation, He wanted to make it special in every way, and so "God fashioned into a woman the rib which He had taken from the man" (Genesis 2:22). When the Bible describes God's efforts in creating the rest of the world, the term *fashioned* is not used. It simply says that He made them or placed them or created them. But when it describes how He made a woman, His Word uses the term *fashioned*.

Webster's dictionary says that the word *fashioned* means to shape, mold, or form. God shaped, molded, and formed woman after His image. He took extra time to fashion all of the intricate details of the woman. Although all of the terms used in Genesis concerning God's formation of the earth imply the idea of creation, only one implies that the Creator took extra time, care, and attention to what He was doing. God *fashioned* woman.

For this reason, I think that as women of the King, we should glory in our existence as the fairer sex. It is so unfortunate that in this day and age our world is full of women who refuse to enjoy who and what they are. We are in such a hurry to work like men, act like men, take positions that are biblically given only to men, and be able to declare ourselves equal with men that we have missed the beauty of being an especially fashioned creature of the most high King. I implore you to discover the beauty of your femininity and revel in it. Enjoy it! It is a gift from God.

How much He must have loved us to give us intricately designed bodies that can bring forth life. We should thank God for that. How much He must have loved us to give us bodies that were created to sustain the very lives that we bring forth into the world. We should praise Him for that. How much He must have loved us to give us the intuition that only women have, the power to influence that only women have, and the emotional structure to give and receive love like that of no other creature on earth. We should be amazed that the Father would do all these things for us; we should thank Him and realize how glorious our position really is. The God of the universe saw that man, His greatest creation yet, still needed help. He gave him a glorious gift . . . you and me!

Many of us not only are unsatisfied with the way that we look physically, but are also upset about our inner selves. We wish that we could be more jubilant, more caring, or less talkative. There are great qualities that we see in others that we wish we, too, possessed.

I have a special friend named Tashara. She is a beautiful woman whom I have admired for a long time. She not only is beautiful physically, but for as long as I can remember she has been a happy person. Rain, sun, sleet, or hail, this woman has a smile on her face and has something positive to say. It is for this reason that many people flock to her and long to be in her company. Growing up with her, I wished not only that I had her incredible size-four body, but also that I could adopt her carefree, happy attitude. I loved her smile and tried my best, at times, to emulate her. However, it soon became all too evident to me that I was not Tashara. It took so much effort to smile like her and to try to have her attitude all the time. It was worse than trying to fit into that size four!

I quickly learned that although Tashara's qualities are extremely admirable and appreciated by all, what makes them so special is that they belong to her. I cannot be like her because I am not her. God wants us to appreciate the way He has made us both externally and internally—body, soul, and spirit. Now I am not saying that we should not look up to and admire others' positive attributes. Often we can use their good qualities as models for re-

44

shaping our own. But to try to mimic someone else's personality is not what God would have us do.

He made you the way you are for a reason. There is nobody else like you on the face of the earth, and He is so glad about that. Psalm 139:13 says, "Thou didst form my inward parts; thou didst weave me in my mother's womb." (KJV) Before you were even born, God knew exactly what He was doing with you. He knew how you would look on the outside and the inside. If you are a quiet person who doesn't like to be in the limelight, then celebrate who you are. Don't feel slighted because you are not always the center of attention. Meanwhile, applaud those who are in the center of attention and admire them for the people that God has made them.

Maybe you are like me—you are the life of the party. You always have to be involved in everything, and whenever you have something to say you say it. I have often wished that I could be like the meek, quiet girls who don't so easily intimidate other people because of their brashness. However, I have to come to realize that God gave me my personality for a reason.

In the same way, there is something that He wants you to do with that personality of yours that you might not do if you didn't have those unique characteristics. Brought under the subjection of the Holy Spirit, your personality can be used just the way it is, so you can do what God wants you to do. Don't wish to be like someone else! God knew you before you were born and was excited about unleashing you on the earth!

Satan's goal is to get us to forget that God made us the way we are for a reason. He knows that if we get focused enough on our weaknesses, we'll never get around to using our strengths for the kingdom of God. He knows that if we are smothered in self-pity, we'll never get up and proclaim the praises of God. He knows that if we are always envying others, we will never learn to love them with Christ's love. Satan is in a war with God and he wants desperately to win. He lost the first battle at Christ's resurrection from the dead. Now he is going to do anything in his power to get us to rebel against God just as he did.

Before he rebelled against God, Satan was an angel. In fact, he was one of God's most prized possessions. There was no angel like him in all of heaven. He was amazing. Unfortunately, he took his beauty a little too seriously and decided that he would do his own thing. Of course that was a big mistake—when God is running the show, you can't do your own thing. So Satan was thrown out of heaven along with all the other angels who wanted to follow him. Today he is known as the "prince of this world" (John 12:31 NIV). Satan resides here and so do we. God made us for the specific purpose of giving Himself glory and proving to Satan that He is in control.

Psalm 8:4–6 (KJV) says, "What is man, that thou art mindful of him? and the son of man, that thou visitest him? For thou hast made him a little lower than the angels, and hast crowned him with glory and honour. Thou madest him to have dominion over the works of thy hands; thou hast put all things under his feet."

If Satan is an angel and we have been made a little lower than the angels, then God is using the lesser to combat the greater on his own turf. God is using us to make it known to Satan that even weak things, even lesser things, when submitted to a holy God, can conquer anything.

Michael Jordan is an extremely talented basketball player who has made millions of dollars as a commercial spokesperson and movie star. Before retiring, this man became the greatest player of all time in his sport. Because of this, he was often asked for his opinion regarding new players entering the league. One season two players were in the running for a spot on the Chicago Bulls team. One of them was a wonderful player with great skill and ability; the other had less talent but was by far a harder worker. This second man had worked hard to hone his skill since he did not have as much pure athletic talent.

Another significant and obvious difference between the two players was that the talented one was very arrogant and cocky, while the other young man was a team player with a humble, upbeat attitude. When asked which player he would prefer to have join him on the team, Jordan responded that although the talented player would certainly bring a lot of skill to the team, he would much prefer the player with less skill who was dedicated and had an attitude that would fit in well with the Bulls.

Use your imagination for a moment and envision you and me playing a basketball game against Satan. Satan has the skill, talent, and sheer power to outsmart us, but he doesn't have all that it takes. We have less skill, and we are certainly not as powerful as he is, but we have the right Coach on our side. Our attitudes must be focused on God. We must be determined to hone our skills by leaning not on our understanding, but by acknowledging Him in all our ways (Proverbs 3:5–6). He has chosen us for His team, and therefore we are on our way to a sure victory!

THE MAKING OF A PEARL

We must rest in knowing that God is on our side. Even more than that, He is for us and is interested in working through us. The almighty King of the universe loves us enough to use us as instruments to fight His battles. He stands tall as our Lord and Leader, and He uses us as His hands and feet to proclaim to a dying world and to Satan that He is in control. He must cherish us a whole lot if He would actually use us that way, because He certainly doesn't need us. It is imperative that no matter what circumstances come your way, whether good or bad, you remember that God is using you in every situation to serve Him and to achieve great things for His kingdom.

God's Word says that He has given us everything we need pertaining to life and godliness (2 Peter 1:3). Everything that you need to be what God has called you to be was given to you before you were born. And whether you feel like it or not, you are a capable woman who is empowered to achieve those things that God has for you. If you were thrust into motherhood six months after being married, remember that God has given you everything that you need to be a great mom. If you were certain you were on your way to an incredible career in politics, law, acting, or singing, and you now find yourself at home with three or four children and a husband, remember that God knew you before you were born. Wherever you are He has given you what you need to be there.

Wherever your path has taken you, your life is no surprise to God. He didn't forget to give you the skills and gifts, patience and talents that you would need to be successful right where you are.

Before you were born, He knew you, consecrated you and appointed you (Jeremiah 1:5–6). Before the foundation of the world God knew who you would be, what you would become, and everything that you would need in order to serve Him in that position.

Sometimes the tragedies of life seem to be outrageously unfair. Maybe you have had what you consider to be a tragic life already, and now you've learned that you've lost your job. Or that your husband is cheating on you. Or that your child is experimenting with drugs. Or that you have "the big C"—cancer.

Haven't you suffered enough already? And now your breast must be removed, and you'll have to undergo the disastrous side-effects that chemotherapy often brings. My sister, nothing that happens to you is a surprise to the Father. He still loves you and has prepared you for this very moment and this very situation. Don't let it overpower you. You are royalty and you reign over your circumstances.

One of the sea's creatures is the oyster. During an oyster's life, a foreign substance of some sort may get caught inside the creature's shell and stay there for a long period of time. This substance can be as small as a grain of sand, but when it gets trapped, the unexplainable happens. The oyster secretes a thin sheet of a substance called *nacre* that encloses the foreign object. Inside this thin sheet, the foreign object begins to change and become reshaped until it is no longer an insignificant grain of sand but a beautiful, shining, costly pearl. The ordinary has now become the extraordinary.

Like that grain of sand, you and I may be quite ordinary, but often God uses something painful and uninvited to change us forever into something extraordinary and beautiful. Our task when uncomfortable circumstances invade our lives is to wrap ourselves in the Word of God. It is filled with a substance that will change us forever and make us into the pearls that we were created to be.

Unfortunately, many of us refuse to accept where we are or what we're facing. But when you believe that Christ knew you before the foundation of the world, then you also know that whatever you have been called to deal with right now, you have also been given the inner strength to survive. Are you single? Stand firm and complete in your singleness; you have been given the grace to be single. Married? Be content with your mate, even if he drives you crazy. Whether you are rich or poor, successful or struggling, young or old, your life is God's gift and He has given you what it takes to flourish in it.

PRIVILEGED TO SUFFER

During seminary, I got to know and love Eric and Yvette Mason with all my heart. I was there as Eric pursued Yvette and believed God's Word to him concerning her. I was there for their engagement and all of the interesting trials that ensued during that period. My relationship with them has touched my life in a wonderful way.

Shortly after they married in December of 1997, Yvette began to experience physical difficulties. She had always been under some strain due to a liver disease, but after the marriage, her problems increased. All at once these newlyweds found themselves at the hospital several times. They were swamped with medical bills, and as seminarians they could not fathom being able to pay them except by a miracle from God.

As I talked with Eric, whom I consider to be my brother, he shared with me some of the pain that this trial had caused them. I can clearly remember Eric saying to me, "We are experiencing things that most people don't experience at all, and if they do it is after twenty-five years of marriage!" My brother in Christ loves his wife and cherishes their relationship. He knows that in spite of the difficulties, this is where he is supposed to be. I tried to encourage him, hoping he understood that God had placed him in a privileged position.

Many men would walk out on their wives in a situation like this. What a privilege that God has chosen to use Eric to show the world a husband who loves his wife as Christ loves the church. Some men couldn't handle the stress, and that is precisely why those men didn't get Yvette. God knew before either Eric or Yvette was born what would happen in their lives. This problem was no surprise to Him. God decided that there was a servant of His to whom He would give the privilege of marrying Yvette. That servant was Eric. Eric was appointed and equipped for the task before the foundation of the world.

The book of Acts tells the story of men who were punished for their belief in Christ and their diligence in serving Him. When Peter was beaten furiously for what he believed and preached, he said that he went away rejoicing because he had been considered worthy enough to be beaten for the cause of Christ (Acts 5:41). Isn't that amazing?

You and I get so upset about any little discomfort that we may have to suffer for any reason. Yet these men felt great joy in knowing that God had deemed them worthy of this challenge. They understood something that many of us forget. They knew that whatever their lot was, God had given them the equipment— internal and external—to handle it. Their self-image was not damaged because of what their life entailed. They didn't feel like victims. They didn't blame God. Instead, they rejoiced because the Lord had allowed them to share His sufferings, and because of what He had predestined for their lives.

God loves you so much. Galatians 4:7 says that you are God's daughter and that you are an heir to the throne. He did more than purchase you and claim you. Just as He did for Jerusalem, He put you in a position that is far more outstanding than anything you could have ever imagined or sought for yourself. He "called you out of darkness into His marvelous light," and for this reason and this reason alone, you are holy, "a chosen race, a royal priesthood" (1 Peter 2:9).

Have you come to understand that you are royalty? As a daughter of the King, you are a princess, with a prestigious position in His royal court. You are a coheir to the riches of Jesus Christ, and His royal blood pulses though your veins. Please remember to hold your head up high, because you have been advanced to royalty. *Remember who you are!*

Consider This

Do you truly believe what the Scriptures say about you?

Do you make certain that others treat you in a way that lines up with Scripture?

How interested are you in looking like and acting like others?

Are you satisfied with the way God made you?

If you could change yourself, where would you start?

What are some ways that God is using you to accomplish His purposes?

What challenges are you facing right now? How have you been equipped to handle these challenges?

God has delivered you from . . .

He has advanced you to royalty by giving you . . .

Prayer of Dedication

God, today, _____, I make the decision to believe that Your Word is true concerning who I truly am. I know that I am in Your hands and that You love me so much that You died for me. I praise You and worship You because before I was even born You knew me, loved me, and prepared me for anything that may ever come my way. I exalt You because I am a beautiful woman who has been created for a purpose. I will decide today to live a life that depicts the position of royalty that You gave to me as a precious gift. Because I am a sinner and because some things have happened in my life that have not glorified You, I admit that I need your help to see myself as you see me. I,

_____, will claim Your promises every moment of every day as I seek to build myself up in You. I trust You and will learn to trust You more and more. Thank You for who You are and for what You have done for me.

In Jesus' name,
Amen

_____
Today's Date

52

Chapter Three

FOR SUCH
A TIME
AS THIS

*G*od sees every woman in His kingdom as a valuable, precious jewel. And what a disservice we do to Him and His royal court when we don't remember who we are. Women who forget their royal position create an invisible barrier between themselves and the potential that Christ has called them to reach. If we don't believe that we are valuable and worth more than the finest jewelry, it will inevitably show in our dress, in our attitude, and in everything we do.

When God created woman He took extra time and attention to make sure that we are the wonderful creatures that He intended us to be. From the very beginning, His special interest in women has been apparent. God carefully "fashioned" us, and we should be proud to be such a special part of His creation. If the Master of the universe was pleased when He'd finished creating us, why shouldn't we be happy with ourselves?

There are three areas of our lives that will demonstrate how we see ourselves and will determine how others see us. These are the physical, mental, and spiritual aspects of our existence. God speaks in His Word about all three, so you can be certain that He intended for us to be concerned about them, too. Our Creator wants us to be well-polished gems, taking responsibility for the various facets of our lives that He has taken the time and effort to create, hone, and polish.

Of course if we pay too much attention to one aspect of ourselves, and too little to another, we become out-of-balance, not well-rounded. In his book, *Finding The Love of Your Life*, Neil Clark Warren gives us insight into being a well-rounded woman. He writes, "Your attractiveness depends on the sum total of your qualities. Your strengths may balance out your weaknesses. A high score in one quality like 'personality' can compensate for a lower score on another quality like 'good looks.' The trick is to maximize your strengths and minimize your weaknesses." We must work on developing ourselves as whole women—making the most of ourselves as women of God's design.

FIT TO BE A QUEEN

As you probably know, in chapter 31 of the Old Testament book of Proverbs, there is an eloquent description of a woman of excellence. This woman provides a model to which every King's daughter should be striving to attain. God's Word says that we "are more priceless than fine rubies" when we are women of excellence. That should be our goal.

Most of the many qualities of the Proverbs 31 woman fall into the three most important categories of a woman's life: the physical, the mental, and the spiritual. Physically, "She girds herself with strength, and makes her arms strong"(v. 17). Mentally, "She considers a field and buys it; from her earnings she plants a vineyard"(v.16), and "She opens her mouth in wisdom"(v. 26). Spiritually, "A woman who fears the Lord . . . , she shall be praised"(v. 30). The amazing woman described in Proverbs 31 is a woman of excellence.

Another intriguing biblical woman is Queen Esther. You probably know the story—Esther was a woman of excellence who put all her best gifts to work in order to serve the Lord, no matter what He asked her to do. She encountered many challenges in her life, yet she was equipped to do whatever the Lord required. She was prepared, as we read in Esther 4:14, "for such a time as this."

Like Esther, you and I have been placed in our own personal scenarios. And no matter how wonderful or awful we think our circumstances are, we are in the midst of them for a reason. God has strategically designed our lives so that we are very instrumental in what is happening around us. God has called each of us "for such a time as this." Like Esther, we have gifts from God that will prepare us for the future.

WONDERFULLY MADE—OUR PHYSICAL APPEARANCE

Although our physical appearance is very important, it is the least important of the three key areas of our life. Proverbs 31:30 says, "Charm is deceitful and beauty is vain." Still, physical appearance is very important to the way we see ourselves and to the way others perceive us.

Now there may be some things that you hate about your physical appearance. I have a very flat nose. I mean, it is flat! When I was born, my mother tried to mold it so that I would have more of a bridge. Her efforts worked a little bit, but my nose is still very flat. This was always a source of much concern for me as I grew up. I hated the fact that I could not change my nose. In my early years, I would put clothespins on it in an attempt to make it more "pointy." Of course, nothing helped.

When I was in high school my obsession with my flat nose continued. One day a young man walked up to me right in the midst of a large crowd of people and said, very loudly, "Priscilla, it looks like someone punched you in the nose and it just stuck there!" Everybody laughed, including me, but I didn't think it was especially funny. In fact, his remark really hurt my feelings because I was so sensitive about that part of my body.

There is probably something you would change about yourself if you could. And in today's world you can! Isn't that great? You can go to a doctor and have your cheeks lifted, your nose sculpted, your lips made fuller, or your hips made smaller. If you've got enough money, you can be completely restructured to look like the beautiful woman that you have always wanted to be. Great idea, right? Or is it?

Have you ever considered what an insult it is to God to change something that He fashioned with His own hands? You are unique for a reason. God made your eyes that way for a specific purpose. He made my nose this way for a reason. He decided to make your hips that wide or to give you those thin lips for His own objectives. He wanted your hair to be thick and straight or long and curly. He designed you the way He wanted you to be. The world does not need another Heather Locklear or Pamela Anderson Lee. The world needs you and me, just the way God made us.

When God made Priscilla and gave me to Tony and Lois Evans, He knew that I would inherit my dad's nose and my mom's high cheekbones. I have often longed for slender, sleek legs like the women in the movies have, but that's not what God gave me. And He wants me to be content the way I am.

Neil Clark Warren writes that reaching your full potential "is best achieved when you start with a deep understanding that you are totally loved just the way you are. If your pursuit of excellence grows out of an appreciation for the way you have been created, you'll grow by leaps and bounds. But if you think you must be different to be loved, your anxiety will mount and your growth will be retarded. You're lovable! And you *can* actualize more of your potential than you have" (*Finding The Love of Your Life*).

My friend Julie grew up hating her nose just as much as I hated mine. She was always teased because of its width. She also had another problem; her hair was short and coarse—considered very ugly by those who knew her. She wanted so badly to have long, thin hair that would move with the wind, and she tried all sorts of different products to change her hair's texture. Predictably, nothing did the trick.

During her college years, this young woman went on a missionary trip to Australia where she was to work with a small tribe. Her goal was to evangelize them and bring them to the Lord. When she first set foot into the camp, she was amazed. She looked around and it didn't take her long to realize that the villagers looked exactly like her, or, more to the point, she looked exactly like them.

The tribesmen stared at her and smiled. The children adapted to her quickly and loved to play with her. The women wanted her to teach them to sew, and they asked her how to cook the way she did. Why was this young woman able to minister to those people so effectively? Because she looked like them.

The people in the tribe had either ignored and scoffed at the other Western missionaries, but they were immensely attracted to this young lady. She was like them! Before the world was formed, God knew what she would require to accomplish His purposes in that place and time. And the very things she hated were the things she needed most.

Of course there are things we can do to make ourselves more attractive—using makeup, wearing nail polish, waxing our eyebrows. But our beauty enhancements should only be accomplished in an attempt to make the most of what God has already done, not in an attempt to change it.

I have competed in eight beauty pageants, and I've been amazed at what goes on backstage. You can't imagine all the little tricks that beauty pageant veterans have devised to make themselves look better. I've seen instant tanning solutions smeared on to keep contestants from looking too white, and I've seen make-up tricks for thinning a face or hips that are amazing. Many pageant girls wrap masking tape or duct tape very tightly around their midriffs in order to give the appearance that they have extremely small waists.

In the last pageant I competed in, I decided that I should try to be pageant savvy too. So I wrapped some masking tape around my midsection. I pulled it as tight as I could so that my midriff would look really small. It worked, but when I had to go out for the swimsuit competition, I discovered that because of the way the swimsuit was designed, everyone could see the tape on my back. I panicked! There is nothing like seeing a woman in a bathing suit with masking tape on her back!

There is very little time between segments during a pageant. You have to practically kill yourself trying to make sure that you're ready to go out on stage the instant your name is called. When I discovered that everyone could see the tape on my back, I had to take the swimsuit down and pull the tape off. Ouch! I had failed to consider what kind of pain this might involve. I'd never before realized that I have little tiny hairs on the small of my back. Well I used to have hairs there—I might not anymore. When I ripped the tape off, I experienced the most intense pain I'd ever felt.

It was awful, but I had to hurry so that I didn't miss my turn in the swimsuit competition. I just had to rip the tape off, around and around and around, and I thought the pain would never end. I finally got it off just in time to hear the announcer say, "And next is contestant number seven, Priscilla Evans." I plastered a fake smile on my face and walked out, valiantly fighting off my tears.

Needless to say, I never tried *that* again. I ended up winning that pageant, but it was my last one, and the tape experience is probably why. My point is that women should make themselves beautiful by enhancing what God has already done instead of trying to change it. There are some things that you cannot change, but many more that you can.

How many times have you looked in the mirror and said, "I need to lose some weight"? Next thing you know, you're out with your friends and you've ordered everything on the menu! I have certainly been guilty of that. Making the best of what God has given us is important, and it takes time and energy. OK, so you can't make yourself any taller, but you can make the best of your 5' frame. Maybe you have a pear-shaped body, but who says that that is bad anyway? And you can always make the best of that shape and wear clothes that flatter you.

Taking the time and energy to make your body the best that it can possibly be is time-consuming and difficult. But it is worth the effort you put into it. You shouldn't let this dominate your life, but it is definitely one of the three parts of becoming a well-rounded woman of distinction. Find out what your ideal body weight should be and start eating right and exercising. Forget all of those diet plans that cost you an arm and a leg. If you are like me, you can't afford them anyway.

People look at me now and think that I have never struggled with weight. They think that I just look great and that being fit must run in my family. Honey, I have to work *hard*. When I graduated from college, I found that I was thirty pounds over what I weighed when I got there. Now, I had to get it in my head that I was never going to make it back to my pre-college weight because our standard weight changes as we get older, but I did need to lose a few pounds. Well, OK. More than a few.

Let me tell you a trick: weight loss is all in what you eat. I have always been an athletic person. When I was in high school, I could eat anything I wanted because I was so active and so young that my metabolism just burned everything up. But as you get older your metabolism slows down, and now that food you were eating when you were younger sits on your hips or someplace else where you don't want it.

To make a long story short, I started eating differently and exercising. Now exercising is important, but you can change your body by changing the foods that you eat. I am a lot more active than my mother is. She works out a lot but not as intensely as I do. Yet she is twenty pounds lighter than I am. You know what the difference is? Our eating habits. I work out more than she does, but she eats less to stay slim and trim.

Weight is a big problem, and many women are plagued by it. However, the Lord is showing me, slowly but surely, that my weight worries are really not only a physical problem. At least part of the problem is spiritual. My struggle with weight has taught me two very important things about my relationship with the Lord.

First, a continued struggle with weight, if it is not the result of some medical condition, is a direct sign that we have not submitted ourselves completely to the Lord. A woman who struggles continually with weight due to lack of self-control in eating will also struggle with other self-control issues, such as immorality and anger. It's not just about our weight. It is about not allowing the Lord to be the Lord of our body.

For this reason, our bodies can become a very negative reflection of the power of God to do magnificent things in the lives of His daughters. How can we minister to drug addicts and tell them to be rid of the disease of drugs when we cannot rid ourselves of our addiction to food? It is so important for us to allow God to gain control of us in this area, and we can only begin this process by praying. We must ask God to forgive us of our arrogance in assuming that He can't handle our weight. Let's invite the same Lord we trust to govern our lives to govern our bodies, too.

Second, I have learned that a consistent struggle with weight represents a consistent struggle with low self-esteem. I have met women who have been told all of their lives that they are worthless. They have come to believe that they have no value, and therefore they truly believe that it is a waste of time to make the effort to lose weight. The problem is that such women are allowing what others say about them to override what the Lord and Master of the universe has said about them. How dare we let the words of others become so powerful that they negate the Word of our Father?

Losing weight isn't the only physical problem women face. Some women need to gain weight in order to become healthier. Some need to make some fashion changes. Some desperately need to get some advice on makeup and hair. I am sure you've run into women whose makeup and hair are so awful that you wonder why they can't tell. Well, before you get too critical, make sure that you are wearing your hair and makeup in a way that is flattering to you and not hiding the true beauty with which God has blessed you.

Queen Esther's beauty got her into the right position at the right time. The king had fired his wife, Vashti, so to speak, and now he was in search of somebody even lovelier than she was. Vashti had been gorgeous, so breathtaking, in fact, that during a party he was having he had ordered his servants "to bring Queen Vashti . . . with her royal crown in order to display her beauty to the people and the princes, for she was beautiful" (Esther 1:11).

The king was a proud husband who wanted to show his wife off to his men's club. But the queen refused to come out, and he was advised to get rid of her so she wouldn't be a bad example to other wives in the land. The king then had a beauty pageant of sorts to find the next queen. The minute he laid eyes on Esther, he was mesmerized by her, and he picked her to rule with him because of her beauty.

Over all of the other women who competed, Esther found favor in his eyes. She had just spent a year beautifying herself for the king, and now she stood before him and won him over because of the sensational way she looked. She believed in herself and knew that she was fearfully and wonderfully made for such a time as this.

An attractive physical appearance has no eternal value whatsoever, but it is a very important and necessary part of being a woman of distinction. Our bodies are what God uses as tools to carry out His will on earth. Our bodies must be as physically pleasing in appearance as possible so that we can effectively minister to others. Some women struggle with disabilities and others with disfiguring diseases. Some, like the young woman who went to Australia, are attractive in one culture and not in another. But we all need to do the best we can with what we have. God wants you to take good care of the beauty that He has given to you. And you can be sure of one thing—you are beautiful in His sight.

The fact is, most of us spend a lot of time and attention on the outer person and considerably less time on what matters most. The Bible puts it this way, "Bodily discipline profits little but spiritual discipline profits much" (1 Timothy 4:8). Esther captured her husband's attention through her looks, but I am certain that she *kept* his attention because of her sweet spirit. When she went before him to request mercy for her people, he probably was not only in love with her for the way she looked, but also because of her kindness and her desire to save her people. She was tender and courageous and had a sweet spirit.

When God created you, He did so with many things in mind. However, the main thing He had in store for you was that you would give Him glory. He wants you to have a relationship with Him that flourishes and is not hampered by sin. He wants us to come to Him and to allow our bodies, minds, and spirits to flourish in His presence. The only way to realize our true beauty is to allow the Father to indwell us and be an immense part of our life and daily existence. And as we grow in Him, He teaches us not only to respect our bodies, but also to be good stewards of our God-given intelligence.

THE MIND OF CHRIST—OUR MENTAL ATTRIBUTES

I believe the popular saying "A mind is a terrible thing to waste" is certainly true. The mind is a wondrous creation. God has equipped us to utilize its fullest potential, although often we don't use it at all. We lessen its importance in our lives by letting it sit on the back burner of our existence. A lot of us went to high school and college, and maybe we even have master's or doctoral degrees, but that doesn't mean that we've really used our minds.

My sister Chrystal is a brilliant woman. She is the type of person who is very astute and loves to master anything that comes her way. I can always remember her using her mind to its utmost capacity. When we were young girls our objectives in life were totally different. She was always studying to make sure that her grades were wonderful. When I did study, it was because Dad or Mom made me. Now I have to be honest with you. I can remember many classes that I took both in undergraduate and graduate school in which I made very high grades, yet I didn't really use my brain at all. I am not proud to admit that, but it is the absolute truth.

My objective wasn't actually to learn anything; it was simply to pass exams. I have an incredible memory, so I could memorize answers until I was blue in the face. I would do an awesome job on the test, feeling so proud that I would be bringing home a great grade for my parents to see. But let me tell you, my prayer was that I would never again have to revisit that information. Once I finished that test I didn't remember anything about it.

Chrystal, on the other hand, knew the information perfectly and worked every muscle in her brain. To this day, she is the genius of our family, and we can count on her to really know information well and to be able to capitalize on that knowledge. The Bible tells us to study to show ourselves approved unto God (2 Timothy 2:15).

To be women of excellence, we need to make sure we are the best we can be. That means we must use our minds diligently and make sure that we are continually learning. You don't have to have a degree to be a smart woman. I know women who have Ph.D.'s and have less common sense than some of their less academically inclined acquaintances. Truly smart women are those who continue to build themselves mentally instead of allowing all of that glorious brain tissue to go to waste. God blessed you with it, so why not use it? Statistics tell us that most people utilize only 10 percent of their mental capacity. What glorious things could we accomplish if we actually would begin to gain access to the other 90 percent?

One of my favorite movies of all time is *Phenomenon,* starring John Travolta. Travolta's character is plagued by some strange occurrence that enables him to do certain things that normal humans cannot do. He can move objects just by looking at them, break things with his mind, and feel the movement of the earth on its axis just by standing on the ground outside of his home. He is a wonder and amazement to all those with whom he comes in contact.

Unfortunately, the reason behind his newfound powers is a brain tumor that has stretched out like a hand all over his brain. The tentacles of the tumor are enabling him to access different parts of his brain that normal people don't have the ability to use. The doctors tell him that he is not really doing anything supernatural but is simply using all of the mental capacity that he has.

The film made me wonder what we would be able to attain if only we would use the massive percentage of our brains that we never seem to take the time to develop. I wonder if we shifted our focus a little and realized that our studying is to "show ourselves approved unto *God,"* whether we would be more serious about using one of the greatest gifts that we have been given.

I have had the privilege of working with Zig Ziglar for the past three years. He is an amazing man who loves the Lord and truly has a heart for people. I remember that the very first time I heard him speak, he said something unforgettable. He explained that we spend a great amount of time in our cars everyday, driving to work, going home, or dropping the kids off somewhere. We spend hours upon hours every year just sitting in traffic. Why not use some of that time to build our minds?

Mr. Ziglar calls his car his "automobile university." In our day and time, a woman can earn a degree in her car. We can learn a different language or enjoy classic novels or hone our math skills while driving to and from our destinations. Instead of listening to endless hours of music, why not listen to something that will actually help us achieve a goal of some sort?

A young lady moved to Dallas without the education that she needed to get the type of job that she wanted. She was turned away time and again because of her lack of formal education. She became very discouraged and settled for a regular desk job at Neiman Marcus. Although she felt bad about her position, she decided that it would not hold her back. But even though she didn't want to be there forever, she didn't have the time to go and get her formal degree from a university.

This woman went to a bookstore and bought some audiotapes that would help her learn to speak Spanish. She got so excited that she went back and bought some tapes that would help her learn French. Then she decided that she wanted to study Portuguese. In two years she had totally mastered all three languages. She now works as the international sales manager of a major company in the United Sates.

All of this occurred because this woman decided that she wanted more out of life and took it upon herself to continue to build her mind. Mind building has nothing to do with high school or college or graduate school, although those things are great. I am talking about a determination to never stop learning.

If you decided to open up your dictionary and learn one new word each day, can you just imagine how much improved your vocabulary would be after 365 days? You would feel so much more confident as you prepared presentations or met with a prospective boss. There is so much out there for us to learn and, as royalty in God's kingdom, you and I are well worth the effort.

When I was growing up, every summer my dad would give us summer reading assignments. I couldn't stand it. I thought that I should certainly have an extended break from the massive amount of studying (memorizing) that I had been doing throughout the year! Of course, Chrystal would read a million books, one right after the other, and I would pick through the assignments one page at a time over the whole summer. We joined the book-reading club at the Polk Wisdom Library in Dallas, and we entered contests to see who could read the most books. Suffice it to say, I never won.

But I remember my father always reading. He spends his spare time studying not only during the summer, but also throughout the year. To this day, if you walk into my parents' house, you are likely to see Tony Evans at the kitchen table with tons of books spread out all over the place along with that same yellow tablet that he always uses to take notes. He is a learn-a-holic—the more information the better.

Often at night you will find him lying in bed with books everywhere, my poor mother looking at the room in disgust as his books and materials clutter her beautiful home. She has made a deal with him: "You can read as much as you want as long as you keep the mess on your side of the room." In spite of everything, my dad has instilled in us a desire to learn. It has even rubbed off on my mom, who is now taking a class at Dallas Theological Seminary. Dad and Mom always wanted us to use our minds to their fullest capacity, becoming the best God has created us to be.

The virtuous woman in Proverbs 31 not only was a beautiful woman, but she was mentally prepared to make sure that things were done well. She used her mind to plan and ensure that her family was well-established in the community. She "considered" land that she would purchase, assuring herself that it would be in the best interest of her family. She had a powerful business sense, and the term *consider* implies that she took her time and studied all of her options before she made a decision to buy. She used her mind.

Esther, virtuous woman that she was, used her mind as well, determining when would be the best time to go before her husband to request mercy for her people. Her decision to do this was largely spiritual, but she had to be smart about the way she went about doing it. You and I are called to be intelligent in our actions. Like the Proverbs 31 woman and like Esther, we must rely on God and yet use the minds He has given us as tools to make wise choices. We must also seek to grow spiritually, so that all aspects of our lives will be brought under the authority of Christ.

THE TRUE MEASURE OF ROYALTY—OUR SPIRITUALITY

In order to be women of distinction, we must make our spiritual lives top priority. It is essential not only to know the Savior, but also to have a relationship with Him like no other. No one can take the place of your God—not your husband, your boyfriend, your children, or your parents. No matter how awesome our loved ones may be, we have to learn that there are some things that only a holy God can do for us.

God wants so badly for His daughters to know Him intimately. He wants us to reach out when we need someone to lean on, and He longs to see that the first place we go in our need is always to Him. He also wants to know that when we are not in trouble and don't need anything at all, we will still turn to Him in praise and adoration just because of who He is. He wants to know us and for us to know Him. The spiritual part of our lives is so important that God gave His only begotten Son's life so that we could experience an unhindered, wholehearted relationship with Him.

Queen Esther was beautiful and smart, but far more importantly, she knew her Lord and knew that she could call on Him no matter what the circumstances might be. What is so intriguing to me about this woman is that even when her physical life was threatened, she depended on an almighty God to keep her.

I think of the thousands of Christians who are persecuted for what they believe. They live every day in fear that they will be killed for their faith, yet they continue to trust in God, who loves them and gave Himself for them. Likewise, Esther trusted in God so much that even though she was frightened for her life she spoke words that showed her total reliance on God: "And if I perish, I perish" (Esther 4:16). Basically she was saying, "Not my will, Lord, but thine be done." She had come to the conclusion that although she was beautiful, her physical being must take a backseat to what the Father needed her to do.

As women who want to follow Jesus and learn to be more like Him every day, we have to make a conscious decision to grow in relationship to God and to know Him like no other. The more we know Him, the more we learn to trust Him. When we trust

Him, then we lean on Him. And when we lean on Him in obedience, He knows that we love Him. Our desire is to love God with all of our hearts, minds, and souls. And this love for Him allows us to realize our royal standing in Him.

The spiritual area of our lives should be the one on which we spend the most time. It should be the epicenter of our existence. The spiritual fruit that we display to the world will be the result of the type of spiritual life that we nurture, so we need to decide what type of fruit we want to grow and then plant accordingly. If you want an apple tree, you can't plant a pear seed. If you want purity, you can't plant pornography. If you want a peach tree, you can't plant an apple seed. If you want kindness, you can't plant grudges. Whatever fruit you want to bear, you have to plant that seed in your spirit.

To maintain healthy, fruitful spirits, we must have daily encounters with the God of the universe. Satan is always on the prowl in an attempt to destroy our self-esteem, which means that we must *always* be on the defensive to guard ourselves against his worst intentions. In order to be prepared, we must have the Sword of the Spirit—God's Word—hidden in our hearts. The only way to have it in our hearts is to read it! Let's commit ourselves to spending time reading the Bible and praying that the Lord will speak directly to us through His Word.

I met my husband while speaking at an event in Dallas. After a whirlwind romance, the time I had looked forward to all of my life finally came. He popped the question and presented me with a ring that I will always cherish. But isn't it amazing how we often look forward to things and then find ourselves a little overwhelmed when we get them? After I got engaged and as my wedding date approached, I was very nervous about this big step.

As long as I had looked forward to this time in my life, I had imagined that everything would be smooth sailing. Boy, did I have another thing coming! That happens to all of us at one time or another—life's twists and turns bring many unexpected things into our paths. But it is when we get to these challenging places in our lives that we learn more about Him and find ourselves reaching out for Him.

God strategically used my anxiety about marriage to draw me closer to Him. One night a few months before the wedding, I lay awake in bed and began to think about all of the intricate details of marriage and how overwhelming it is to pledge your life to someone else. I was brought to tears at the realization that I was really scared to death to take this step.

Now I am awestruck that God would send someone so wonderful in my life as Jerry (more about that later), and that God would allow me the privilege of illustrating His love for the church with this relationship. Then, however, all of the fear and doubt that any normal woman has welled up inside of me and, at times, caused me to become very nervous about the lifetime vows that I was about to take.

One night I was driven to my knees in a hotel room in Rockport, Illinois. I cried out to God and gave Him all of my fears once again. I laid my relationship with this man at His feet and prayed again as I had been praying throughout the whole process, "Lord, if this is not Your will, then You stop it."

This is exactly what God wants from you and me. He wants to know that our main interest is that His will be done. As the tears fell from my eyes, I could imagine God cupping His hands on my face and saying, "I am in control." It is so comforting to know that He is, indeed, in control of every situation.

After I prayed, I got back up in the bed and tried to sleep. Instead, I found myself being prompted by the Spirit to pick up my Bible, which had been sitting on my side table untouched all night. I didn't know what to read, so I lay there in the dark of night thinking about how comfortable I was and how much I didn't really want to turn on the light.

But I had just prayed that the Lord would help me to hear His voice. I had just prayed that He would take away my fear. I wanted reassurance that I had heard God's voice and that He would speak clearly to me about the wedding and our marriage and all that lay ahead of us. So I reluctantly got up, turned on the light, and flipped open my Bible. I read the first thing that fell open. This is what it said:

At this also my heart trembles, and leaps from its place. Listen closely to the thunder of His voice, and the rumbling that goes out from His mouth. Under the whole heaven He lets it loose, and His lightning to the ends of the earth. After it, a voice roars; He thunders with His majestic voice; And he does not restrain the lightnings when His voice is heard. God thunders with His voice wondrously, doing great things which we cannot comprehend. (Job 37:1–5)

. . . And God says,

Have you ever in your life commanded the morning, and caused the dawn to know its place; that it might take hold of the ends of the earth, and the wicked be shaken out of it? (Job 38:12–13)

Where were you when I laid the foundation of the earth! Tell Me, if you have understanding, who set its measurements, since you know? Or who stretched the line on it? On what were its bases sunk? Or who laid its cornerstone, when the morning stars sang together, and all the sons of God shouted for joy? (Job 38:4–7)

A smile slowly found its way across my face. It was very obvious to me that God was saying that He had everything under control and that my worry was not necessary. He was showing me that His voice was not so small that I have to listen hard for it, but that, instead, it is as obvious as thunder and lightning. He made it clear to me that He wants me to know Him, to know His voice and therefore trust Him and depend on Him to supply my need and take care of me. If He can make the world work, then surely He can take care of me!

No matter what our fears may be, He wants us to know that, just like any good father, He is always there. He longs to have fellowship with us, His precious royal daughters. He longs to see that the very first place we look to for help and reassurance is in Him. And He longs to meet us in our joy and our celebration, in our heartaches and our sorrows, in our sin and our shame, so that He can do His wonderful work in our hearts, making us more and more suited to His royal court.

God is the great Renovator. He seeks to renovate us from the inside out. All of the physical and mental preparation and beautifying in the world is irrelevant if our spirits are not in tune with God. So He seeks to make us all over again. If we allow Him the opportunity, He will do so, and the changes in us will be immediately apparent. And when He decides to make us over, He does a major overhaul.

About three years ago, for my parents' twenty-fifth wedding anniversary, my mother had their entire house renovated. They had decided to do major remodeling so they could have what they needed without moving. I was in college for much of the time that the renovation was taking place, so a lot of the changes happened while I was gone.

One weekend I decided to drive home from school for a short visit. When I got home, everything was torn up. There was construction equipment, tools, and boards lying all over the place, and the entire front door was gone. As I drove up, I looked at the house in shock. I waded my way through the mess and called out my parents' names. Through all the dust I finally made my way back to their bedroom. It was even more torn up than the rest of the house. It was obvious that they couldn't be living there. What a terrible mess! I called my sister and found that they were staying with her for a week or so until at least the bedroom was fit for habitation.

This is exactly the kind of work Christ does. Sometimes He decides that the renovation of our lives, from the inside out, will be so severe that we'll certainly have to move out of our comfort zone. He may want to deal with our physical bodies. He may want to motivate us intellectually. He may have new spiritual lessons for us to learn. But when the Master Renovator shows up for work, watch out! God is in the process of making you what He wants you to be—body, mind, and spirit. He has created you to be a woman of excellence. You are an adornment to His royal court. You are becoming a beautiful jewel in His crown—*"for such a time as this."*

Consider This

What action steps can you take right away to change your appearance for the better?

What can you do to learn to appreciate the beauty and uniqueness that God has given you?

What are you doing to be a continuous learner?

What interests you the most on an intellectual level?

What changes would you most like to make in your spiritual life?

Are you more concerned with your physical appearance than with your spiritual appearance? Explain.

Prayer of Dedication

Lord, there are several areas of my life that I need to work on so
that I will feel better about myself. I need Your consistent help to
improve the _____, _____,
and _____ areas of my life, and I am
trusting You to help me make the changes. I have tried to do
these things in my own power before, but I want You to give me
Your strength this time. In the name of Your precious Son Jesus,
I submit my total being to You and ask You now to take control
of every area of my life. No longer will I allow
_____ to control me or my attitude about myself.
I refuse to allow Satan to have any hold on me. I often feel defeated because _____.
However, I know that because You had the power to rise from
the dead and to heal many people when You walked on earth,
You can help me in such a time as this.

In Jesus' name,
Amen

_____

Today's Date

REMOVED FROM THE GARDEN

The young woman opened her eyes and lay quietly for a moment. She wasn't quite sure what to do or say, or whether to do or say anything, so she just lay there in silence. Her eyes hurt because of an intense brightness—what was that distant object that shone so brightly? Her mind raced with thoughts of both excitement and anticipation. Where was she, who was she, and how had she gotten here?

The fresh, green scent that comes after rain lingered in her nostrils. She had never smelled anything like it. Suddenly, she felt a sensation, a tingly feeling that caused one finger to move. She moved another finger, and another, until her whole hand was now in front of her, within eyesight. It blocked the brightness of the sun.

She then lifted her head ever so slightly and looked down at her body. It was very beautiful indeed. As she continued to move, she found with great astonishment that this object belonged to her, and when she wanted to move it, she could. What were those ten things at the base of this beautiful piece of art? Did they belong to her?

Obviously somebody had bestowed upon her an extraordinary gift, but all of this was so new, so unique. She had never seen anything like it before. She was sitting up by now, and her attention was so fully captivated that she hadn't even noticed the long, colorful creature that was coiled nearby. Only when it moved away did it capture her attention.

Just before it vanished, her eyes met its eyes, and she was momentarily captivated. Those eyes looked back at her and seemed to tell her things about herself—things that made her feel proud and important. The strange attraction between her and the creature seemed almost magical. She heard something behind her and glanced around, then she looked back toward the colorful creature, but it had vanished.

She lifted her head and drew in a breath. She had been so consumed by her initial waking and by the creature that she hadn't even noticed her surroundings. There were gorgeous trees and vines everywhere. Plants and flowers abounded in color and beauty beyond belief. She was captivated. Above her was a magnificent blue canopy, containing beautiful white pillows that she longed to touch. In fact, she wanted to touch everything.

Just then she heard His voice. "Eve!"

She knew nothing of her surroundings, but she somehow recognized that voice. No matter where she was or what she was doing, she would always know that voice.

"Yes, Father," she replied. She was almost too excited for words. "Where am I?" she asked. She breathed a sigh of relief, knowing that He was there. Now she knew that she was all right. It was part of who she was to trust her Father.

"All that you see," He explained, "I have given to you. You are my beautiful daughter, and you are worthy of many gifts. I will use you to give Me glory in this new place that I have created. There is another one like you who will come to you. I have made you to be a suitable helper for him. You and he will become one flesh, and your life together will be filled with joy because I will always be with you. I will come and walk with you in the Garden and speak with you often. You are My little girl and the gifts that I have given you are special. Take care of them for Me. If you need anything from Me, just call out to Me, for I will never be far away.

"But remember this—from the fruit of the trees of the Garden you may eat, but from the fruit of the tree which is in the middle of the Gar-

den you shall not eat. Don't even touch it! I have placed everything else within your power, and there is nothing else that you cannot have. I only keep those things from you that will do you harm . . . because I love you so dearly."

Eve was content and comfortable, because everything she needed she had. She did not understand all that was taking place, but she felt peaceful and happy. Her Father had given her so many beautiful gifts— gifts that she did not deserve. He must really love her and care for her. What a magnificent Father He was!

She continued walking into her new, unknown world, pondering the Word that her Father had spoken. He had said that someone was coming to her. Who was He talking about? Was it the colorful creature she had seen before? If so, where had the creature gone? So many things were unanswered, yet she believed every word her Father had spoken.

She heard the soft sound of feet against leaves and turned around. In the distance she saw a most elegant figure walking toward her. His shape was much like her own, and she had not seen anything like him in the Garden. In an instant she knew that this was the one that her Father had promised. Now she was not alone.

Eve rested and waited and reflected. She had been given so many wonderful gifts in such a short period of time, and now she could not wait until the next gift appeared. She sat for several moments. Nothing. She waited a little longer, looking around her as if she expected another miracle to take place at any moment. Still nothing. She began to be bored. She needed something to do.

She looked around to find something of interest to occupy her attention, and all at once her eyes locked on the colorful creature that she had seen before. Its long body was coiled in a tree nearby—the tree in the middle of the Garden. She was once again drawn to the eyes that seemed to tell her so much about herself. She walked toward the creature, and this time it opened its mouth and spoke to her. Its words met her at the point of her need. "This tree upon which I rest will bring you joy beyond belief. You will have all that your Father has. In fact, you'll be just like Him if you'll simply eat of this delicious fruit."

Eve's first inclination was to turn and walk away, for her Father's voice had spoken very clearly to her concerning this. But instead, she lingered. She couldn't resist the temptation to come closer and see what the serpent was talking about. Her Father was wonderful—what could possibly be wrong with being just like Him? At first she resisted, but then she tasted. She disobeyed. She disregarded her relationship with her loving Father. The consequence was evident. She and her new husband would now be removed from the Garden.

WOMAN—THE CROWN JEWEL OF CREATION

God created His most precious gift on the sixth day of His creative process. He spent five days forming the earth and all that it contained, and then He brought forth man from the ground. He designed and formed Adam and breathed into him the breath of life.

However, after all the work that He had done, He looked down and discovered that His work with man was not yet complete. He saw that "It is not good for the man to be alone," (Genesis 2:18) and so He created a helper suitable for him—He created woman. Have you ever heard that you should save the best for last? This is exactly what God did.

Woman was the vehicle that Satan would use to bring sin into the world, yet in His infinite grace and mercy, God would use this same vehicle to bring the Savior into the world—the One who would redeem the world from its sins. This woman who ignored her husband's leadership and decided to do what she thought was right was forgiven, and God loved her despite her wickedness. Women are special in the sight of the Creator. He knew what He was doing when He created a helper for Adam. He saved the best for last.

God gave Eve everything she needed when He created her. He gave her not only external things to make her content, but internal things that would keep her satisfied. She had a wonderful place to live where there was harmony and peace. All of the animals loved her, and in God's new creation they lived together in unity.

God wanted the best for His daughter. He wanted her to have the most wonderful existence that He could provide for her. He placed her in a serene atmosphere in which He cared for her personal well-being. He gave her an awesome husband who loved her dearly. She had a plush garden in which to live, work, and play. She had it all.

Eve also had the sort of relationship with the Lord that each of us should strive to attain. She had the opportunity to walk with Him every day. She experienced His love and attention firsthand. He guarded her and her husband and led them in a life that was nothing short of paradise. He was much more than their God; He was their Friend. I suspect that they had discussions about their lives and what direction He wanted them to take. Eve was in perfect relationship with this God whom she served and with the husband He had given her.

God had created humankind for one reason and one reason alone—to give Him glory. This was exactly the way He had planned it. It couldn't get any better than this. Adam and Eve were His obedient children whom He loved. He gave them everything that they wanted and needed. Surely they didn't really need access to that one tree, did they?

We women are just like Eve in that God decided that the world needs us. Have you ever thought about this? God looked down on earth after He had created everything else, and He determined that the world just could not make it without you. He decided that He would not allow you to be aborted. He determined that even though some of your friends have not lived to see this day, earth is still in need of you. Although you may not deserve to live, He continues to give you the gift of life in hope that you will utilize that life to its fullest potential.

God loves you dearly! He wants the world to experience you, your uniqueness, your gifts, your talents, and your abilities. He has gifted you with your race, your gender, and your culture. He determined that you were born at the day and time when the earth most needed you. It was no mistake. You are God's gift to the world. You are a crown jewel of His creation.

THE OLDEST TRICK IN THE BOOK

Unfortunately, anything that God wants to do that is pure and holy and beautiful, Satan wants to destroy. God has given you a beautiful relationship with Him in which to grow and bear fruit.

Satan wants to destroy that. He will do anything in his power to remove you from the flourishing garden of your relationship with Christ.

Satan knows that as a woman you are susceptible to the tricks that he has up his sleeve. One very old trick is this: The devil seeks to get you to *do*, *be*, or *have* anything that God has not called you to do, be, or have. Not too amazing is it? You see, the devil knows that if he can get you to strive for something that is not ordained for you, then inevitably you will not get it. When you don't get it, you will automatically think that there is something wrong with you. In actuality there is nothing wrong with you; it's just that the thing you are striving for is not something that God has called you to do, to be, or to have!

Are you following me? How about that guy that you have been striving your hardest to be with, and he still isn't paying you any attention. Or that job that you have been trying with all of your might over and over again to obtain. Or that promotion that you have been lying, cheating, and stealing to get. Maybe you can't get them because God has not ordained them for you.

Of course when we don't obtain things like that, our first inclination is to look at ourselves and say, "What is wrong with me? Am I not smart enough, cute enough, or dignified enough?" Sometimes we look at the woman who got what we wanted, and we say, "What does she have that I don't have?" This is where jealousy is born.

There's nothing wrong with you! That thing was just not meant for you, so—hard as it is—let it go. The devil wants you to strive for things that aren't meant to be yours. He wants you to sweat and cry and make yourself miserable over people, places, and things that always seem out of your reach. He wants you to think that you can't get those things because you are just not up to par. And he'll do everything in his power to put them in your path so you'll strive for them, only to fail miserably.

Satan played this game with the very first woman on the earth—my girl Eve. She was content in the Garden of Eden. She had her home, her God, and her man. She lacked nothing at all. She lived in a serene place that she had literally been brought to by God. She knew she was in the will of God for her life because she walked with Him and talked with Him every day. If something was missing in her life, she didn't know it. She was content. Everything that she needed had been given to her by the almighty God, and she was in perfect peace. I'm quite sure that she believed in herself and her value as a woman because of her relationship with the Father.

Leave it up to Satan to attack a young woman who has a great relationship with the Father. In fact, you need to understand that the closer you are to the Lord, the harder the devil will attempt to trick you and snare you in his traps. Satan knows that outside of your relationship with God you will not be able to realize your royal potential and beauty in the King's court. Your self-worth is found in your closeness and nearness to the Father, so Satan wants to see that destroyed.

PLOTS AGAINST THE KING'S DAUGHTERS

You see, there are certain women that Satan knows he can fool. There are some women who are so worldly minded that he knows he already has them under control. But he feels challenged by those of us who dare to think that we are truly God's daughters. Proud as he is, he devises his plans specifically with you and me in mind. He will work extra hard to destroy our testimony—and us.

The devil wanted to take advantage of Eve's position. The nature of the entire world rested on her shoulders, and he wanted to corrupt it with sin. It is also important that you notice that Satan did not go to Adam; he went to Eve. He knew that as a woman, she was the gateway to the future. Satan knows where true power lies. I know that men are the leaders. They are the heads, but we are the necks that turn those heads! So the trick of the devil is to get us to do, be, or have anything that God has not called us to do, be, or have.

God told Adam and Eve that they could eat of anything in the Garden except the Tree of Knowledge of Good and Evil. Of course, that's the tree with which Satan seduced Eve. Genesis 3:13 says that the devil "deceived" her. That same serpent wants to deceive you too. He wants to get you interested in doing things that God doesn't want you to do.

Satan wants to get you involved in things that are of no eternal purpose so you'll be too busy to enjoy the things that God really wants for you. What are you doing right now that is keeping you from enjoying what God has for you? Satan will turn this plot around in a number of ways. For example, he often tries to get us so bothered by the one thing we have been commanded by God not to do, that we spend far too much time thinking about it. Ultimately it distracts us from obeying God in other areas.

We become so preoccupied with certain restrictions that God has placed on our lives that we forget, just as Eve did, that those restrictions are for our own good. Without them we would be in big trouble. Sometimes single women and men are so consumed with "trying not to have sex," or at least trying not to go too far, that they are not enjoying the gift of being single. They see physical intimacy as something that they have to spend inordinate amounts of time and attention trying to avoid. Although they should indeed avoid having sex outside of marriage, singles often get so upset about the fact that they cannot have sex that they miss out on what God does want them to be doing in their relationship—learning about one another.

What joy there is in simply enjoying what God has for us right now. But in order to do that, we must not be consumed with what He has asked us *not* to do. The rate of adultery in our country has skyrocketed in recent years, and this can, at least in part, be attributed to a simple thing: Satan has dangled the carrot of singleness before the eyes of those who are married, and they have been carried away by curiosity and craving.

If you are single, he tries to cause you to become powerless in your singleness. If you are married, he seeks to make you powerless in your marriage. If you are working in the ministry, he wants you to yearn for more money. If you have children, he wants you to long to be free to do whatever *you* want, at the risk of abandoning your family. Whatever it is that God has *not* called you to do right now in your life, Satan will do his best to entice you with that very thing. Beware!

TEMPTED TO TAKE CONTROL

The second trick of the devil is to get you to want to be something that God has not called you to be. Satan went straight to Eve because he knew how powerful it would be for her to make a decision without consulting her husband first. It was his strategy to get Eve to take the lead. He knew then and knows now that a woman without a man's covering is deadly.

Satan will do everything in his power to get us to take the lead in our homes. He wants to make us resent our husband's position of authority so that we will begin to usurp it. He can't wait to put his plan in motion. Women need to pray for God to renew a spirit of submission in their hearts. Now, I know that you just dread to hear that word, but it is through our submission that we are liberated, healed, and restored. We can rest when we are submitted to a man who is submitted to the Lord.

I really feel sorry for guys. They have a whole lot of responsibility. Not only do they have to be in control of themselves and their spiritual and physical lives, but when they marry they are now responsible for us too, not to mention our children. However, God created men with the innate ability to take on this responsibility. He did not create women the same way. We were made with the innate desire to follow the lead of a male.

We live in a generation that tells us women to do our own thing in our own way and to leave men out of the equation. Most of us would not say that we are feminists. We certainly don't agree with most feminist principles, but unfortunately, although we don't realize it, many of us cherish one major feminist ideal: we don't want to submit.

If you are single, I encourage you to take note of this in your life. Begin to pray that God will mold you and prepare you for the submissive role that you will eventually have to take in order to be a godly wife. Women are waiting longer to marry nowadays, and in all those years of singleness they live on their own and pay their own bills. Single women make decisions for themselves as to where they will go, what they will do, and with whom. They certainly don't have anybody telling them what to do, whether they can go out, or when they need to be back in. They've become microwave queens, cooking for one without needing to be concerned about anybody else's favorite foods.

Single woman, what makes you think that when you walk down the aisle, all of a sudden you are going to have a spirit of submission bestowed upon you? Do you honestly believe that you'll suddenly want to do whatever your husband asks of you? Girl, please! You are going to feel very rebellious.

You may be all right at first, but that old spirit of independence is going to creep out and catch you and your new spouse by surprise. He will wonder what happened to the sweet, compliant woman that he married. You will wonder who on earth he thinks he is. The only solution will be submission on your part.

Begin to let God work in your heart in regards to submission right now. Why? Because Satan will take advantage of any little part of your heart that has a tendency to want to be what God has not called you to be. Satan wants us to try to lead our homes and our men because that is exactly the opposite of the Lord's design.

If you aren't married, find a godly man under whose leadership you can receive counsel about important decisions and concerns. Every woman needs to be under male leadership. If you are married, of course your leader will be your husband. If you are single, ask God to send a man, such as a pastor or church leader, into your life who will provide a godly covering for you until your husband arrives.

CRAVING WHAT WE SHOULDN'T HAVE

It's amazing how that one tree looked so tantalizing to Eve—so desirable that she could not resist. She had the enjoyment of all of the other trees in the Garden, but she just couldn't get her mind off of that one thing that she wasn't supposed to have. Isn't that the way life works? The third trick of the devil is to get you to want to have something that God has not called you to have.

Satan wanted Eve to eat the fruit from the forbidden tree. And sin multiplies; and one thing always leads to another. When you were a little girl, did you ever notice that when you told one lie, you had to tell another to cover up—then another and another? This is the nature of sin. And sin yields consequences.

After Eve and Adam had taken and eaten the fruit, God pronounced a judgment on them. In Genesis 3:16 one of those judgments is on the woman: ". . .Your desire shall be for your husband, and he shall rule over you." If you read that too fast, you won't catch the importance of what it says. One of the consequences of Eve's sin is that she would desire attention, affection, and love from her husband. Instead, he will simply rule over her. If this doesn't prophesy the nature of relations between men and women, I don't know what does.

If you are like most women, you have probably noticed that men in general don't feel like they are on an emotional roller coaster when a woman doesn't want to go out with them. They don't lie down on the floor and cry, or call up all their friends for advice, or teeter on the brink of a major emotional breakdown. However, women do. There are some single women who embarrass themselves with their desperate attempts to gain a fellow's attention. I am quite sure that this is because part of the curse given to women is that we would desire love, attention, and affection but that it would not be returned.

Because of God's judgment, you and I tend to desire things that don't desire us. We want to have men who are not right for us. We want a job that is not meant for us. We want possessions that aren't appropriate for us. When we don't get these things, we are emotionally distraught, and this is exactly what Satan wants. When we lose sight of Christ and put our sights on what we cannot have, we begin the process of being removed from the garden. When we want something that is not meant for us, we are distracted from those things that God wants us to have. Our goal must be to hear God's voice and to trust Him to lead us. No matter what we want to do, to be, or to have, we must trust that He knows what is best for us.

One day I had to travel to a distant city to speak. I don't remember where I was going, but I will never forget the plane ride that took me there. When I fly, time goes by quickly because I work on my laptop or read some information to prepare myself for what I'm going to say. I am often so engrossed in what I am doing that I don't even look up when the flight attendant comes by. I usually don't take my eyes off my work until a jolt shakes the plane and lets me know that we have landed.

This particular flight was very memorable. About an hour into the journey, the plane suddenly dropped. There was no gradual decent, no nice easy way down. We simply plunged. Luggage tumbled into the aisle. Passengers screamed. People who had been walking fell to the floor. Everyone was very shaken up. I sat still, completely startled, not knowing what to expect next. Along with everyone else, I was quite afraid.

A few moments after the drop, the pilot's voice came across the PA system. He cleared his throat and announced very calmly that, although he was very sorry, he hadn't had any choice in what had just happened. He explained that he had received an urgent call from the control tower saying that we were flying on a collision course with another plane. There would have been a major calamity if we had not immediately dropped away from our original flight pattern. After the announcement, we were still pretty shaken up, but having heard the reason why we had to drop, we understood. We didn't like the discomfort of the drop, but we certainly preferred that to a plane crash.

Sometimes the Lord has to shake us up a bit to move us off a collision course with disaster. He is the control tower, and He is the only One who has a full view of our lives. There may be something that you were desperate to do, be, or have that He did not allow for you. The sudden bump that He used to shake up your life may have been very uncomfortable for you, but I'm sure you would prefer a minor disruption to a major crash.

God wants most of all to protect His daughters. We need to put everything under subjection to Him because He sees the whole picture. He knows when the Enemy wants us to *do* something, *be* something, or *have* something that is unsuitable for the royal women in the King's court. If we are walking with Him in the beautiful garden of our relationship with Him, He will guide us and guard us. He will lead us into safety. He will steer us away from the plots and plans of that colorful, slithering creature who —after all these years—is still making promises he can't keep.

Consider This

How has Satan attempted to remove you from the beautiful relationship you have with your Lord?

In what specific ways does Satan seem to have victory over you?

What are you trying to *do* that might not be God's will for you right now?

Who or what are you trying to *be* that is not what God intended for you?

What are you trying your hardest to *have* that is obviously not what the Lord wants for you, at least right now?

What blessings could you be missing out on because you are only interested in what you want and not in what God wants for you?

Prayer of Dedication

*I come to You humbly, dear Lord, and ask for Your forgiveness.
In many ways Satan has removed me from the garden that I
share with You. I often don't spend time with You because there
are so many things going on. I know, however, that nothing that
I have to do, not _____,
_____, or _____,
is more important than being with You. I know that Satan is trying to deceive me in many ways. Unless I hear and recognize
Your voice and know what You are telling me to do, I may suc-
cumb to the temptations that the devil sets before me.*

*Lord, my goal for the future is to be _____.
However, I submit that to You. I ask that You would give me the
mind of Christ and that I would want to do only what You want
me to do. Lord, I sometimes want to be a leader in my home
with my husband or in other positions in which I am not to
lead. I pray that You would help me to come underneath the
leadership You have set in place for me. Help me not to want to
be anything that You have not called me to be.*

*Finally, Lord, I really want to have _____,
_____, and _____.
However, today I submit those things to You and ask that You
only allow me to have what You want me to have. I am totally
Yours, Lord, and I do not want to be tricked by the deceptions of
the devil. Lead me in the path of righteousness in the name of
Your great Son, Jesus.*

*In Jesus' name,
Amen*

_____
Today's Date

Chapter Five

JEWELS
IN THE
MUD

o you ever feel worthless? Do you ever look in the mirror and wonder what anybody sees in you? Satan would love to deceive as many women as possible into believing that they are good-for-nothing. If he can make us feel as if we have no value, he has found a way to keep us from fulfilling our destiny as women in the King's court. He knows very well that women are powerful beings, the gateway into the future.

When we women don't value ourselves, our sense of worthlessness filters down to our children. It affects our friends. It impacts the men in our lives. It damages our relationships with all kinds of people. It influences those around us because they learn from us. Too many women are imitation jewels who will, unfortunately, raise their children to be the same unless some significant changes take place. And Satan loves it; he has successfully influenced a generation of women who are truly diamonds, to believe that they are not valuable. So they act like cubic zirconium. Remember you are the real thing.

I am so grateful for my mother. She did not allow Satan to take advantage of her, and because of that her four children and her granddaughter have benefited. We have clearly seen her awareness of her place in God's kingdom, which has given her a great sense of dignity and godly pride, and she has instilled a similar sense of dignity and pride in us. It is imperative that we not allow Satan to strip us of knowing our rightful position in Christ.

Maybe you suffer from low self-esteem. Perhaps you were abused as a young child. Maybe you were made fun of when you were younger and the repercussions of that have continued. Maybe there were circumstances beyond your immediate control that challenged your proper sense of self. It wasn't your fault that your mother called you names that now haunt you. It wasn't your fault that your father or uncles abused you physically or emotionally.

But, my friend, it is your fault if you have not recovered from that by allowing the Lord to heal you. I know that that may sound harsh. But Scripture reveals that we have the power in Christ Jesus to rid ourselves of the effects of the past. By God's grace, we don't need to cling to the guilt and shame that keep us from reaching our full potential. Maybe you cannot forget, but you can recover and move on.

Did the man you truly loved leave you for some other woman? Have you been passed over again and again for a promotion that you richly deserve? Did you overextend yourself financially and do you now have to face creditors and the threat of bankruptcy? Honey, it is time to get up and move on. Don't let the past strip you of your promised future happiness.

Jesus "came that [we] might have life, and might have it abundantly" (John 10:10). He wants you to live an abundant life that is full of beauty, peace, and contentment. He doesn't promise happiness, but He does want it for His children. It is a gift.

I'VE FALLEN AND I CAN'T GET UP

In the Dallas Galleria we have a store called Imposters. If the name of the store didn't give it away, you might never notice that every piece of beautiful jewelry sparkling in the showcases is fake. Every twinkling ruby, every glittering diamond is just an imitation. Those faux gems look like the real thing, but they are not.

If you went to any other jewelry store in the mall and bought a real diamond, I am certain that you would appreciate it a lot more than whatever you might buy at Imposters. Why? Because it would be more valuable to you. You would have spent more money on it. You would be more careful with the real thing because it is rare and valuable and precious.

The same rule applies to us—if we don't believe that we are real jewels, worth an enormous amount, then we will not value ourselves the way we ought to be valued. You have to realize that you are not an imposter. You are not cubic zirconium in the King's crown. You are the real thing. Have you forgotten that you have been bought with a very precious price?

The reason most people remain in the tragedies of the past is that they do not think they are worth the effort that it takes to move on. They do not realize that they have the power and, yes, the responsibility to get up and get going. If you fell into a mud puddle, you wouldn't stay there, would you? You would want to get out as soon as possible and clean yourself up. You would want to go home and take a shower and put on different clothes.

Or is it possible that you might stay in the mud just because you want to be there? Maybe there is a certain comfort in being so dirty that you can't get any dirtier. And if you get up out of the mud puddle and don't want to get cleaned up immediately, it might be because you want everyone to know that you fell in the mud or because you were comfortable there. Does one of these apply to you?

Again, maybe it is not your fault that you are in the mud. Maybe someone else pushed you into the mud puddle a long time ago. But why are you still in there? Are you just sitting there reminiscing and allowing the mud to strip you of your true beauty? If so, why?

Have you ever dated a guy and noticed that he has the same characteristics that caused you to break up with a previous boyfriend? Are you constantly engaging yourself in relationships with other women that are not healthy for you? What is the true cause of your inability to quit smoking or to stop using drugs? It would be so easy to blame somebody else for your present situation, but

God has called His women of the kingdom to a higher standard. He does not want us to live in the pain of the past but to get out of the mud and experience the blessings of the present and the future. He wants us to experience the joy of the Lord. Joy and blessings cannot be found in the mud. We need to get up, get out, and move forward.

THE CLOTHES OF ROYALTY

Maybe you have gotten up out of the mud puddle of your past, but you are still wearing your old, mud-covered clothes. By that I mean that you are addicted to self-pity. You have pity parties for yourself, and you like to invite people over so they can pity you because of your mud-covered clothes. You are no longer in the puddle of financial debt or a broken relationship, but you still have the clothes on so that everyone can see and recognize how strong you must be to have gotten out of that puddle. There is only one problem with that: your identity is being ruined by the puddle of the past that is keeping you dirty.

Does the mud of abortion, debt, or divorce still cling to your skin and your garments? Every time you peek at yourself in the mirror, does your self-image take another nosedive? Naturally, your friends know that your self-esteem has been demolished by the mud of your past. But they probably aren't going to tell you that. They are just going to pity you right out of the self-esteem that is rightfully yours.

I don't want to attend any pity party, especially one that is about me. Why? Because as God's chosen women, we should want others to see us moving about our lives with a noble bearing. They should wonder how we can walk with our heads lifted so high. Our goal should be to exhibit the fruit of the Spirit in such a way that others just want to come and take a bite out of us and experience the good taste of our lives.

Now I am not some saint who has never fallen in the mud. I have had to change my clothes several times. In special seasons of prayer, I have requested that the Lord remove my filthy garments from me and dress me in spotless, new clothes that will remind both myself and others of my worth and value.

What about you? Isn't it time for the mud to come off? The God of the universe wants to clothe you in robes of righteousness. He has already given you a new beginning, a new name, and a new purpose for living. He will also give you a new wardrobe that is fit only for a woman of royalty. Wear His clothes with dignity and don't let the mud hide their value. Why walk around looking like a commoner when you are a jewel in the King's crown?

HOT WATER—FIRST CYCLE

I have a very rambunctious niece. She is a work of art. She is always getting into something that has no lasting effect at all except for the dirt that it leaves on her clothes and body. Whenever I spend time with her, it reminds me to think twice about starting my own family!

Kariss and I love to hang out together, and I find joy in spending time with her. One of our favorite pastimes is roller-blading. She and I love to get on a path near my home, take off, and skate to our hearts' content.

Although it is fun for us now, I remember the first time we tried roller-blading together, and it wasn't especially enjoyable. I guess I overestimated the time and distance that she should have been able to handle at seven years of age. I was quite sure that she would be just fine skating the same distance that I cover when I roller-blade on my own.

My sister drove us in her car and dropped us at our starting point. Not too long after we began, Kariss began to get tired and upset because her feet and back were hurting. I really felt bad for her, but I just couldn't do anything about it. There was no way to get back except to stick to our original plan and roller-blade back to my place. I quickly began to see that this trip was going to be miserable.

After I'd tried everything in my power to encourage her to continue, I gave up and told her that we could walk the rest of the way. Now you have to get the whole picture here. It was a cold day, and the later it got the colder it got. Not only was it cold, but it had also been raining a lot during the past few days. There was mud everywhere!

We came to the first big mud puddle, and you guessed it: Kariss thought that this was the most wonderful thing she had ever seen. She ran right through it. Suddenly the smile was back on her face. Once again she was having the time of her life. She ran and jumped and had a blast. Well, anyone who knows me and the relationship that I have with my niece knows that I am a big pushover. It doesn't take long for Kariss to get her way with me.

Next thing I knew, I was splashing around in the mud like a seven-year-old. We hopped and skipped and ran. And then we fell —both of us—right into the huge puddle. Well, I figured that there was absolutely no point in trying to stay remotely clean then. If Kariss was happy, so was I. We splashed and splattered our way through all of the mud puddles on the way home and had a great time in the process.

By the time we got home we were a mess. I undressed Kariss and myself. I threw all of our clothes into the washing machine and switched the dial to hot water. Needless to say the clothes were still very stained (maybe I should have used Tide!) even after they'd been washed. I washed them a second and a third time, and they still weren't quite clean. They obviously needed some extra attention and care—and bleach! Detergent alone wouldn't do the trick.

Sister, you and I also need extra care and attention to remove the stains of our past. We wonder why it is so difficult to undo the damage when we have been in the washing machine so many times. We go to church, we sing in the choir, and we try our best to hang around godly people, but for some reason we just can't seem to get rid of the stain that is left from the mud. Isn't it amazing how something so fun can leave a stain that lasts so long?

HOT WATER, CLOROX BLEACH—SECOND CYCLE

My home church, where my father is the pastor, begins every year with an event called the "solemn assembly." It is a week during which everyone in the church is asked to fast their dinner meal and television for one week. The purpose of the event is to invite God to be an integral part of the life of the church in the new year, and to request that He intervene in miraculous ways in the individual lives of the congregation.

May I suggest to you that fasting might be the "bleach" that you need to remove the stain from your life? The Bible says that there are some stains that only come out by fasting and prayer. Fasting is when you give up satisfying the needs of the flesh in order to satisfy the greater needs of the spirit. Fasting proves to God that you are very serious in your desire for spiritual renewal.

At the beginning of 1999, during our solemn-assembly week, our church had a wonderful time in the Lord. Many miracles occurred right before our very eyes. One of my requests to God was that He remove from me the bondage of sin and guilt in my life. He is continuing to answer me. When we fast, according to Isaiah 58, God wants "to loosen the bonds of wickedness, to undo the bands of the yoke, and to let the oppressed go free, and break every yoke" (v. 6).

When God knows that we are truly serious about Him, He does things in our lives that we never thought possible. He can change our circumstances in a hurry because He is the God of miracles. And if your life is anything like mine, then you need a miracle to fix the mess that you've made by playing in the mud for so long. For those of us who need the most help, He makes this promise:

Then your light will break out like the dawn, and your recovery will speedily spring forth. And your righteousness will go before you; the glory of the Lord will be your rear guard. Then you will call, and the Lord will answer; you will cry, and He will say, "Here I am." . . . Then your light will rise in darkness, and your gloom will become like midday. And the Lord will continually guide you, and satisfy your desire in scorched places, and give you strength to your bones and you will be like a watered garden; and, like a spring of water whose waters do not fail. (Isaiah 58:8–11)

Perhaps hearing the word *fasting* makes you just a little nervous. I can remember sitting in the pew and listening to the announcement concerning the week of solemn assembly and getting a little antsy. No dinner? How was I supposed to do that without dying?

Please remember that fasting is not just a religious game. You must recognize some great spiritual need in order to fast with the correct intentions. There is nothing miraculous in the giving up of food itself. Giving up food is simply a diet. What makes fasting different is *the reason* you give up the food. The reason should be spiritual need.

We can also choose to fast from television, chocolate, or any other thing that is gratifying to our flesh. If you are married, the Bible talks about fasting from sex in order to hear God's voice more clearly (1 Corinthians 7:5). We need to fast from something that is important to us, and for most of us that important thing is food. It bears repeating—fasting will get God's attention so that He sees how serious you are about changing your life and removing the mud stains for good.

RINSE AND SPIN—THE LAST CYCLE

Once we have washed away the mud of the past, we have to work at staying out of mud in the future. How unfortunate it would be to spend all that time cleaning up only to fall back into another puddle or, worse yet, the same puddle as before.

Author Portia Nelson writes:

> **Chapter one**
> I walk down the street
> There's a deep hole in the sidewalk
> I fall in
> I am lost and I am helpless
> It's not my fault
> It takes a long time to get out
> **Chapter Two**
> I walk down the same street
> There's a deep hole in the sidewalk
> I pretend I don't see it
> I fall in
> I can't believe I am in the same place but
> It's not my fault
> It takes a long time to get out
> **Chapter Three**
> I walk down the same street

There's a deep hole in the sidewalk
I see it there
I fall in
It's a habit, my eyes are open
I know where I am
It's my fault
I get out immediately
Chapter Four
I walk down the same street
There's a deep hole in the sidewalk
I walk around it
Chapter Five
I walk down another street.

Are you still walking down the same road? How many times have you fallen into the same hole? Are you hoping that the mud puddle won't be there anymore? I can promise you that it will. Let's stop trying to prove to God that we are strong enough to walk down that street without getting caught in the same old mistake, hindrance, or sin. We aren't proving anything to God except that we are ignoring His still, small voice.

A washing machine fills to the brim with water and uses the power of the detergent to clean the clothes that are inside. After a few moments of rigorous rubbing, twisting, and turning, the tub becomes still and the water begins to drain. Along with the water that drains from the machine, the dirt that was removed from the clothes in the washing process drains as well. The machine then refills with new, fresh water and cleanses the clothes a second time. If it simply re-used the water that had been in there before, then it would simply be re-depositing the waste that it had just taken so much time to remove. What of waste of energy that would have been; to remove the dirt and then deposit it once again onto the fabric. Once it rinses with new water, the machine furiously spins and shakes the excess dirty water from the fabric. It wants all remnants of the past gone for good. The rinse cycle is of utmost importance because no matter how much washing and bleaching you do, it serves no purpose if you just put the dirt back on. We have to rinse the dirt off and shake off any remnants of the mud. We never want to see it again.

Iyanla Vanzant is a very skilled author and counselor who has been a regular guest on the Oprah Winfrey show. Her book *In the Meantime,* although not spiritually founded on Christian principles, does offer us some advice for finding the love we desire in our lives and in our relationships.

One of the things Ms. Vanzant emphasizes is that women need to be aware of their patterns of behavior. What is it that you do over and over again that always seems to land you in that same old mud puddle? For some that pattern involves falling madly in love with men who do not love them back, causing sorrow and frustration. For others the pattern is a desire to have things that do not belong to them, creating attitudes of jealousy and envy. Still others follow the pattern of anger in their lives. They cannot develop healthy relationships because they have so much anger contained inside—anger that they refuse to release to God.

Patterns like these enslave us and strip from us our true potential. The Lord will show you your pattern if you just ask. He says plainly, "If any of you lacks wisdom, let [her] ask of God, who gives to all [women] generously and without reproach, and it will be given to [her]" (James 1:5). God will reveal so that He can heal.

PREPARED FOR THE STORM

I have had the great privilege of traveling all over the United States and speaking to women about their value in the eyes of Christ. In the process, it has dawned on me how very little we really think of ourselves. My heart aches to convince God's women that they no longer need to allow the mud of the past to strip them of the beauty of the future. Too often Satan outsmarts us in this way. He knows exactly what street we are heading down and which specific puddle will cause us to fall miserably and mess up our new, Christ-given clothes. He keeps an eye on us, knows us in the most intimate way, and understands exactly how to trap us.

When I competed in national cheerleading in high school competitions, we used to watch tapes of ourselves and of our opponents so we could compete with them more successfully. This is exactly what Satan does to us. You and I are on one team and Satan is on the other. Satan and his team watch your tapes. They sit back and watch the unfolding of your life, analyzing your strengths and weaknesses. The forces of darkness want to determine how they can outsmart and outmaneuver you whenever possible. They want to win!

Your enemy is trying to determine what street he needs to maneuver you down and what mud puddles he should have waiting there. From watching our tapes of past performances he knows that he can get some of us with jealousy. He knows that he can trip others up with immorality. He knows from watching your tape over and over again that he can catch you in the mud puddle of pride, discontentment, or guilt. He will watch your tape until he finds some way to defeat you. He wants you in the mud and he wants you there soon.

When we were saved, we were not promised a life filled with only happiness. We were never told that we wouldn't have to deal with mud puddles again. The world with all the problems it posed before we were saved is the same world that we must live in afterward. We are still susceptible to the same troublesome temptations that always seemed to find us.

Sometimes God allows our clothes to be muddied for one reason and one reason alone: "That [we] may know Him" (Philippians 3:10). He is deeply interested in His relationship with us, and sometimes that means that we have to go through something terrible in order to appreciate Him. Often we do not come to know Him until we are in dire need of Him. It is during this time that we learn to lean on Him, and we also learn what we are really made of. Some of us think that we are wonderfully spiritual. Yet when the storms of life come our way, we are quickly swept away.

I facilitate a small Bible study group on the campus of Southern Methodist University in Dallas. Every Monday night of the semester, I meet with a group of young women and we spend time sharing in the Word and praying together. Before we begin we often have a time of praise to the Lord when we share the awesome things He has done for us.

One week at that Monday-night Bible study, I heard an interesting story from a student whose name is Elaine. Elaine and her family had recently taken a trip to Mississippi to be with other family members. The weather was bad throughout the time they were there, and they were careful to plan enough time to drive home safely, taking note of the terrible conditions. They had heard that a storm system was bringing tornadoes with it, but they were fairly certain that they could beat it. They began their drive back to Dallas. Although they did beat the tornadoes, they ran into some severe flooding along the way.

Elaine told us of the fear she felt as she watched small cars being swept away by the floodwaters. The little compact cars were not heavy enough to keep their tires on the pavement when the deep waters surrounded them. Elaine was scared, but she felt fairly safe because just three weeks earlier she and her family had purchased a Chevrolet Suburban. Their large utility vehicle was well prepared for just that kind of weather condition. Although at times Elaine could feel them momentarily floating rather than driving down the road, because of its massive weight and size their Suburban was not swept away.

Our spiritual lives are often like that. We can always tell if our relationship with the Lord is up to par by the way we handle the flooding. We may have sports car type lives that are cute and flashy and turn on a dime, but when the storm comes we are easily swept away. Cute little sports cars are not built to handle the storms of life. The Lord wants to build us into heavy-duty Suburbans that can stand the test of rocky terrain and turbulent weather.

FIGHTING TO WIN

In actual fact, our battle is not against the elements. Galatians 5:17 says that our flesh and our spirit are at war against each other and that both are battling to win. God's Word explains that the flesh sets its desire against the spirit and the spirit against the flesh. This battle over you and your self-esteem is no walk in the park—it is a major fight to the very end. If God's Spirit wins, you will have won your ability to experience abundant life in the here and now. *But don't take the battle lightly.*

Our battle becomes more obvious to us when we are standing on the edge of a mud puddle and are at the moment of decision. Will we choose to turn around and walk down another street, or will we once again find ourselves wallowing in the mud as we have so often done before? We stand on the edge, arguing and debating, and most of us have a really hard time putting our feelings aside and doing what we know is right.

Our minds race back and forth between good and evil. On the one hand, we hear the words our mother and father spoke to us when we were little, telling us to focus on Jesus. Yet when we look at the mud puddle, it looks so inviting. For a moment, the fact that it is going to stain our expensive God-given clothes of royalty doesn't really matter. Everything in us says that the mud will feel *so good.* We are torn between curiosity and righteousness. What do we do? Who do we allow to win the battle? Who gets the victory this time?

Often for me the battle has been overwhelming. I have been brought to tears because the desire to do wrong tempts me in unbelievable ways. Paul writes about his struggle in Romans 7:

> I am of flesh, sold into bondage to sin. For that which I am doing, I do not understand; for I am not practicing what I would like to do, but I am doing the very thing I hate. But if I do the very thing I do not wish to do, I agree with the Law confessing that it is good. So, now, no longer am I the one doing it, but sin which indwells me. For I know that nothing good dwells in me, that is, in my flesh; for the wishing is present in me, but the doing of the good is not. (vv. 14–18)

Paul, the godly and faithful apostle, explains in this passage how desperately he wants to do righteousness. He longs to live a life that is holy and acceptable in the eyes of God. Yet he just cannot do it. Something continues to pull at him and cause him to do the very things that he doesn't want to do. I've felt that way all too often, haven't you?

Why does it happen? Why are we so easily led astray, captivated by things that are unholy, unjust, or unrighteous? Paul says that the "flesh" has a hold on us that refuses to let go. Although we desire to finally rid ourselves of the mud, we just cannot seem to do it. The flesh is the culprit. Although once we accept Christ we are born again and righteousness now indwells us, we are still surrounded by our external covering that is infested with the disease of sin.

The flesh covers us. It is with us wherever we go. We cannot run or hide from it. As long as we are on this earth we will be attached to our fleshly bodies. And the only way to outsmart the flesh is to have a spirit that is stronger. The only way to overcome the demands and temptations of the flesh is to have an internal system that is stronger than the external.

The reason we fail miserably in many ways is because our spirit is overcome by the power of the flesh. It is that simple. We can talk all we want about living the victorious Christian life, but if our flesh is a monstrous giant that simply steps on our puny, undernourished spirit, we can be sure that we will be defeated every time.

There is a very important reason why our flesh is so strong: we feed it too well.

Suppose you have two pets. You feed one excellent, healthy foods and make sure that he gets his rest. But you refuse to feed the other and you give him none of the things that he needs to be healthy. You will quickly see that one will be stronger than the other. This doesn't happen because one was born with better genes or growth potential. It happens because of the attention that you pay to one and the way you ignore the other.

Likewise, we often spend so much time attending to the flesh that it becomes strong and overpowering. We then wonder why we keep failing in our spiritual life. We watch all kinds of movies and fill our mind with the dirt we read in the romance novels we love, and then we wonder why we continue to fall into sexual immorality. We spend all our spare time walking around the mall, looking at every kind of expensive merchandise imaginable, and then we wonder why our credit cards are maxed out and our finances are a disaster. We rehearse arguments and nurse grudges, and then wonder why we keep having ugly confrontations with people. We simply feed our flesh and ignore our spirit. We must reverse the situation by nourishing our spirit through prayer, fasting, and continuous Bible reading, while starving our flesh so that it can be overcome.

This process of denying the flesh and pursuing the heart of

God is called "walking by the Spirit." It sounds simple enough, but it requires a moment-by-moment, hour-by-hour, day-by-day pursuit of God and His righteousness. Remember that there is a battle going on and, as Galatians 5:16 and 25 says, "Walk by the Spirit, and you will not carry out the desire of the flesh," and "If we live by the Spirit, let us also walk by the Spirit."

Walking is one of the most elementary parts of our physical activity. Most people do it every day. After several weeks of walking we learn how to do it well, and we rarely think about what we are doing. It just comes naturally. We walk by placing one foot in front of the other. In the same way, we learn to walk by the Spirit. Our goal is that it should become so routine for us that we are able to do it naturally. We must learn to walk in faith by placing one spiritual foot in front of the other.

Whenever we face a spiritual challenge or some temptation that could potentially destroy us, we must right then place all of our faith in Christ and in His promise to us that there is no temptation that is not common to man (1 Corinthians 10:13). And when another temptation to sin comes our way, we must place all of our faith in Christ and His promise that He never gives us more than we can bear.

This process of walking by faith is a continual system of placing all of our faith on one spiritual foot at a time. We will find that when we do so, we make more spiritual progress than we've ever made before. Galatians 5:17 does not say to sprint, or to hop, or to skip, or to jump in the Spirit, but to *walk*. God wants us to place all of our faith and trust in Jesus—one step at a time.

I mentioned earlier that our goal is to deny the flesh, to learn to spiritually walk in such a natural way that eventually it will requires less and less effort. Although this is our goal, I have some disturbing news for you. *It is impossible not to struggle with the flesh while we are here on earth.* We will always have to remain cognizant of our walk in the Spirit. Paul gets so frustrated that he says in Romans 7, "Wretched man that I am! Who will set me free from the body of this death?" (v. 24). He wonders if he will ever be rid of the struggle to free himself of the bond of sin. He sounds like so many of us, tired of finding ourselves in a mud puddle.

I can imagine what you are probably thinking: "OK, Priscilla, that sounds really great. I do my best while I am on earth, but I won't be able to really overcome this flesh thing until I get to heaven. So what about today? I need something for the here and the *now*."

I have great news. Romans 7 ends with the assurance that through Jesus Christ our battle with the flesh will be over when we see him face-to-face. But Romans 8:1–2 goes on from there. It says, "There is therefore *now* no condemnation for those who are in Christ Jesus. For the law of the Spirit of life in Christ Jesus has set you free from the law of sin and of death." Amen! You and I have all that we need right now to keep us going until the day when we see Him face-to-face.

MINING FOR REAL GEMS

You know, there's a lot of similarity between a woman emerging from a mud puddle and a fine jewel being brought forth from the heart of the earth. Precious gems are found deep beneath the earth's surface, often in dark, muddy mines. A newly discovered jewel wouldn't look very attractive to you if you saw it before it came into the hands of a master craftsman. It might be mistaken for a rock or a clump of dirt or even a piece of dried mud. But to a jeweler, who is able to determine where its faults are, how to cut it into the strongest possible shape, and how to polish it to dazzling brightness, its value is evident from the moment he sees it. Eventually it is cleaned, polished, cut, appraised, and prepared for a beautiful setting in a necklace or a ring or a crown.

Imitation gems do not go through the same process as genuine stones. They are manufactured by the thousands, so there is nothing rare about them. They are all identical, so there is nothing unique about them. They are not carefully analyzed before they are cut and polished because there is nothing really special about them.

The women of God who grace His court are brought forth from the earth with great expectation and joy. Because the Jeweler knows a precious stone when He sees it, each of us is identified as a priceless treasure. Then the work begins. If you are still a little muddy, don't despair. The King sees what is hidden beneath the mud. He is at work in your life to make you shine like a star. He's at work in your life now and will continue to polish and perfect you as long as you live. And "He which hath begun a good work in you will perform it until the day of Jesus Christ" (Philippians 1:6 KJV). King Jesus knows that you're no imitation. He made you Himself, and you're the real thing.

Consider This

List the sins or past experiences that you have not forgiven yourself for.

List the people whom you have not forgiven for what they have done to you.

If you have been in sin, are you still in any way participating in that sin? Explain.

What specific steps can you take to walk down another street?

Do you truly believe that God has forgiven you and loves you because you are His daughter?

In what ways do you allow the flesh to defeat the Spirit in your life?

What important thing could you fast so that you can be removed from the mud puddle and rid yourself of the stains for good?

Prayer of Dedication

Father, I know that You love me and are willing to forgive me for things that I have done that have been contrary to Your will. I admit that I am a sinner and that I have deliberately taken part in things that are not of You. Father, I also admit that I don't understand why things like_____, _____, and _____have happened to me, but I will trust You with them.

Sometimes I wallow in the mud of my past, and I know that it is Satan's tool to keep me down. I want to realize the full potential that I have in You, and therefore I release anything that I am holding onto that is not pleasing to You. I forgive _____, _____, and _____. They have hurt me, but still they are Your children. I ask You to help me to cleanse my heart of all bitterness, anger, and resentment toward anyone who has caused me pain in the past. I know that the only way I will flourish in You is if I get out of the mud, allow You to clean me off, change clothes, and redirect my path. Today, I commit to do that. I ask that You honor my commitment and guide me with Your power.

In Jesus' name,
Amen

_____

Today's Date

105

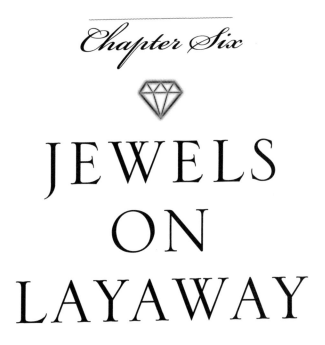

Chapter Six

JEWELS ON LAYAWAY

THE RELATIONSHIP FACTOR

There were two tears floating down the river one day. As they floated down the stream they spoke to each other. The first tear asked the second tear, "Where did you come from?," and he said, "I fell from the eye of a woman who loved a man and lost him." Then the second tear asked the first tear, "Where did you come from?," and he said, "I fell from the eye of the girl who got him!"

What does the most damage to a woman's self-esteem? Abuse? Parental rejection? Immoral decisions? Financial failure? Divorce? Disease or disfigurement? No, of all the damage done, certainly unhappy relationships with men are the number one thief of female self-esteem. A painful relationship with a man can rob us of our sense of worth. And believe me, I know it's true.

Women were created to be relational creatures. The Lord said, "It is not good for the man to be alone; I will make him a helper suitable for him." When God decided to give the man some help in tending the Garden, He created woman. A major reason for our existence is to be in relationship with the male.

Of course, the feminist movement will teach us otherwise. Feminist activists encourage us, "Do your own thing, make your own decisions, and never let a man slow you down." But the Bible makes it clear from the beginning that our primary purpose is to come alongside a man and to assist him.

That is precisely why dating and having boyfriends can become such a painful cycle for us. We long to be in a relationship in which we are needed, loved, and cherished. But ironically, the very thing we were created to do, the very thing we want to do most, is the very thing that often contributes to our low self-esteem.

One reason for this is the way we prepare ourselves for relationships. Most of us don't spend our time waiting for God's chosen man by reading His Word, meditating upon His ways, and praying for His wisdom. Instead, we read novels, go to movies, and get hooked on soap operas. We buy into a fantasy world, and we secretly hope that it will one day become the portrait of our lives.

We see those hot, steamy romances on the screen, then look at our boyfriends or husbands in disgust. The awesome-looking men on those shows know all about romance, sweeping women off their feet with charm, flowers, candy, and eloquent words of affection. Meanwhile, the women never seem to age, even though they have four children and three grandchildren, never work out, eat out every night, and are starting on their fifth marriage. We build such close ties to these fictional characters that we find ourselves wanting to be like them. Then when our real lives fall short of our unrealistic expectations, we are miserable.

ONE VERY PERSONAL HEARTACHE

I was once in a relationship with a man whom I considered to be God's greatest gift to me. Kenneth was wonderful. He was intelligent, handsome, and godly. His passion, like mine, was ministry, and to me we seemed like a perfect match. We first met during my senior year in high school and then ran into each other again while I was at the University of Houston studying broadcast journalism.

Kenneth was a ladies' man. All the girls thought that he was the most amazing thing that the University of Houston had ever seen. He was in the most popular fraternity. He was kind and handsome, and just about every girl in the school was longing to go out with him.

When I was a freshman, I entered the Miss Black and Gold beauty pageant. Since Kenneth's fraternity sponsored the pageant (black and gold represented their fraternity's colors), I spent a lot of time around the frat guys during rehearsals and meetings. It was a lot of fun, especially after I won the pageant. This meant traveling with the fraternity brothers and doing several speaking engagements with them. I also moved up to the next level of the pageant, which was the statewide competition. I won that pageant and the regional pageant, and I placed second runner-up at the national pageant.

All of this traveling brought me into close relationship with the young men in the fraternity. They were like my big brothers—all except Kenneth. He and I began to "like" each other. We spent a lot of time together, but our relationship only lasted about a month before he decided to move on. I was a freshman and he was the "big man on campus." I thought I was really something, and I really liked him a lot. But even though my heart was crushed, I moved on and dated other people, as did he.

At the beginning of my senior year in college, Kenneth came back into my life, and he set out to win my heart. By that time, I had more rules and regulations when it came to dating, and I was determined that he would have to follow them all. When he wanted to get serious, I told him that he had to go talk to my father in Dallas.

Let me tell you, it is no small thing to talk to Tony Evans about dating one of his daughters! But Kenneth drove to Dallas to see my father, and I was impressed. He bought me roses and did all the things any guy would do to let me know that he was very serious about me. He won my heart and we began to date. It was an exciting relationship, and I was sure it would end in marriage.

Not long after our relationship began, Kenneth told me that he felt sure he had been called into ministry. This made me both excited and scared. I was excited that we would be doing the Lord's work together, and scared that we would be poor! Most of all, I was thrilled and proud to be in a relationship with the most incredible man I had ever met.

After graduation we had some decisions to make. I had already been considering seminary, and by now he was too. I knew for sure that my choice was Dallas Theological Seminary, since that was my father's alma mater. There was no other choice to make except whether I would start school the following semester or wait until the spring.

Kenneth had to decide which seminary would be the best for him. I really hoped that he would choose Dallas, and after much deliberation he did. We both moved to Dallas and began school. He pursued a four-year degree in theology while I went for a two-year degree in biblical studies. I was excited about the fact that he would be near me and that we could move toward marriage together.

Two months after we began our studies, Kenneth broke up with me. He explained that he wasn't so sure that he wanted to get married. Only one month earlier we had been so content. In my diary I had written:

September 6, 1996—*Kenneth moved here a week ago. We are doing really well. We went to his family reunion and it was very nice.*

On the day he broke up with me I wrote:

October 11, 1996—*Life is so interesting. My, how it takes its toll. Today, Kenneth and I broke up because he is not ready to move on in our relationship. He is having a love affair with seminary right now, and I just don't fit into that, and I may never fit into that. I really love him and want to marry him, so I wonder how this will work out.*

Thus began a string of breakups that continued throughout my two years at Dallas. Kenneth's intention was not to break my heart. He was just consumed with other things, and I didn't fit into the picture. Why would any woman want to hang around a guy who was making it obvious to her that the season was not right? But that's exactly what I did.

March 17, 1997—*It's a brand-new year. A long time has passed. Kenneth and I have broken up again. Basically over the same issue— marriage. I miss him so badly. I am hurting so badly because I want him more than anything else. I miss him, but I am sure that the Lord knows what's best for me. I am trying so hard to be patient and not call him.*

April 8, 1997—*Kenneth and I finally talked and have gotten back on speaking terms. Things are friendly between us.*

May 14, 1997—*Today, I read Elisabeth Elliot's whole book,* Passion and Purity. *It was amazing. I am missing Kenneth so terribly, but the Lord has shown me through that book that I have been totally out of line when it comes to my relationship with him. I am always the initiator, always. That is not the way that it is supposed to be. Kenneth has kind of stopped talking to me, and I don't know how to act. I called him three days ago, and since then we haven't talked. I told him that I missed him.*

The mystery is not there. He knows too much, including the fact that I miss him. He called me a few weeks ago to tell me not to get bitter toward him. I know he still cares, but he just seems to shut down. That drives me crazy. But being alone drives me to God, and that is exactly what He wants! Getting alone with Christ, what a phenomenon. I almost don't realize my worth when I am in positions such as this. I begin to think of all of the reasons why Kenneth wouldn't want to call me or be with me. I am going through so many transitions, about fifty million of them at the same time. Last week I told Kenneth that I needed to talk to him. I just knew that he was going to get back with me. He never did. That hurts so badly. I wonder what he is doing and thinking right now. Not knowing what the future holds is torture. But it is in not knowing that we trust in God to know.

I took a six-week trip to North Carolina during the summer of 1997. I was devastated about my relationship with Kenneth. But I still hung onto the hope that he would come back to me.

June 25, 1997—*I am still praying about my relationship with Kenneth. I would still love to marry him. Before I left for my trip to North Carolina on June 4th, he kissed me and told me he loved me. He called me here to check up on me. We have talked several times. I will continue to be prayerful while I am here.*

July 25, 1997—*I am back in Dallas now. About two weeks ago Kenneth told me that I was definitely his wife! We were in Church's Chicken having a little lunch on July 10. We talked and he told me that I am definitely the one for him. He told me that he is considering moving to Washington and starting a church and he wants me there to do ministry with him. I tried to play it cool, but I really wanted to jump out of my skin with excitement. This is what I have been waiting to hear from him.*

The whole time that I was in North Carolina, I was praying that when I returned something like this would happen! This is exactly what I wanted, but I haven't heard from him since then. He is still pretty distant. I still haven't called but I am breaking down slowly but surely. Twice I have gone up to the school where he works with some other seminary students, claiming to see if "anyone wants to have lunch," but really I have only wanted to see him. I have really been breaking down.

I saw him today and he kind of acted very nonchalant, so I asked him on my way out if he was ignoring me. Of course, he said that he wasn't. I guess since he spilled his guts to me, I expected things to change and kind of be patched up. That doesn't look like it is going to happen. But anyway, back to my excitement. He said that the Lord has made it clear to him that I am the woman for him. We talked a little bit about kids and stuff. He said that no woman could deter him from me. He said that when he asked me to marry him, if I wasn't ready then he would just wait until I was. I was in seventh heaven!

August 1, 1997—*Kenneth and I took a trip to Houston to visit his family. We had a good time. He told me that he loves me very much.*

August 4, 1997—*Kenneth and I had an argument on the way home from visiting our friends. He says that we don't need to be together anymore. That makes me so upset. I kind of flew off the handle, because he always wants to break up. His solution is always to end the relation-*

ship when there is a problem. It doesn't seem like he loves me enough to forge through anything.

August 5, 1997—*Today was horrible for me, but I am determined not to call him. At 12:30 P.M. today, I got a voice mail from him telling me that he wanted to meet me later. He came and picked me up and took me to Bachman Lake. He apologized to me and told me that he wanted to listen to me again and really hear and understand all of my complaints. I told them to him. He listened. He admitted his failings and where he was weak and stubborn and then explained to me that when he says to me that we don't need to be together that it never means indefinitely, but just for now.*

We walked around the lake for two hours and talked. He explained to me that he wants to be by himself for two years and then he will marry me after he has spent some time alone with God. I can respect that. Kenneth knows and believes that I am his wife. I believe that he is my husband. But for the next two years he wants us to be separated so that he can take care of his business and so that I can take care of mine. I love him and feel like two years is much too long. I feel like maybe I am more worried about the possibility of losing Kenneth in two years. And why doesn't he want to marry me now? What is wrong with me that he doesn't want me now? What am I supposed to do for the next two years?

Kenneth couldn't seem to make up his mind about me. We would break up for a while, and then he would be back in my life again. It was obvious to me and everyone else that there was something seriously wrong. He clearly did not love me the way that he should have. But why was I allowing myself to be hurt, let down and disappointed again and again? I was wasting so much valuable time that I should have been using to learn and to prepare myself for ministry.

August 9, 1997—*It is Saturday morning and I have decided that today will be a day of fasting and prayer. I want the Lord to speak to me about things that I need to change in my life and things that I need to do to make me a more godly woman. I am also praying for direction in my relationship.*

I spent the majority of that semester crying over Kenneth. He wasn't talking to me despite his promise that I was to someday be his wife.

August 18, 1997 A.M.—It is only 10:28 A.M. and I have cried five times this morning already.

August 29, 1997—I woke up this morning thinking about Kenneth. In fact, I had a bad dream about him and woke up, my stomach feeling queasy, and I couldn't go back to sleep. I cried while running around the track this morning. I just called Kenneth. I feel like I made a big mistake in doing that. I asked him if we could meet tonight. He said that we could. I can't believe that I am going crazy over a man who doesn't want me. This is terrible. Surely this is not the way it is supposed to be.

September 3, 1997—Today has been pathetic. I cannot stop crying now. I saw Kenneth today and once again he was so cold to me. This hurts so badly. I just laid out prostrate on the ground and cried my eyes out to the Lord. I am hurting so badly. I hope that God comes through with a miracle soon.

September 6, 1997—Hold your head up high, Priscilla! You are a priceless jewel that is being refined by God in preparation for a lifetime with Kenneth.

September 11, 1997—Cease striving and see the salvation of the Lord.

September 18, 1997—Kenneth is still very distant. It hurts but I guess I'll get over it. I care deeply about him.

September 30, 1997—I am definitely not a very gracious waiter. I have been teaching the girls in my Bible study group to wait, but I don't think that I am doing a very good job of it.

October 4, 1997—Kenneth and I spent some time together last night. We went to a mixer at the school and then talked until six o'clock in the morning. Mostly about ministry, but we talked about us too. It's good to finally be talking to him again.

October 5, 1997—Today Kenneth called and we spent some time with some people from his home church. It was fun. After church we went out to eat with those folks. I wonder if the Lord is trying to open up the door for us again.

October 17, 1997—God is telling me to do His will, and that means giving Kenneth up right now. That really frustrates me so much because that means totally giving Kenneth up and waiting on God to give him back. But He won't give him back until I give him up. I cried a lot tonight. I am deciding today to give him up for six months and see what the Lord does.

October 29, 1997—I was hoping that this wouldn't happen. I have just decided to let God work on me for six months, and wouldn't you know it, Kenneth is calling and wants to hang out and the whole nine. Kenneth has wanted to talk about marriage a lot lately. He brings it up.

November 4, 1997—Kenneth and I spent the weekend in Houston together. We had a great time. On Saturday night, we had a serious discussion about our relationship. He said that he wants me to seriously consider marriage before his last year of school. On December 31 (my birthday), he wants us to make a final decision about whether or not we will be married. We are supposed to really be in prayer over this for the next two months. It was great to have that discussion with him. My heart dropped from my chest into my feet. I already know that I want to marry him. I don't need two months to pray about it.

December 13, 1997—Kenneth and I are a mess. This is turning into a three-ring circus. Today our friends got married. After the wedding we had a discussion because he was acting strange. He said he is uncomfortable with our relationship. The groom's vow to his bride today was great. Why doesn't Kenneth want to make that vow to me? What is wrong with me? I can't imagine walking down the aisle to another man. Anyway, we talked after the wedding, and he told me that we need to separate. I couldn't believe what I was hearing. Here I was about to tell the man of my dreams that I would marry him, and he wants to break up only two weeks before we make the decision. Kenneth and I are over. He doesn't want to make the decision on the 31st.

January 23, 1998—Today Kenneth told me that he no longer feels the same way about me. He basically said that he doesn't love me anymore. WOW!

What was the problem here? Why did I continue to hang on to Kenneth so desperately? Why didn't I seem to care whether or not the man I loved valued me as a priceless ruby? In retrospect, the answer is simple: I did not value myself. I was the problem. I didn't esteem myself highly enough to recognize that I deserved the kind of love a Christian man is supposed to have for a woman. The Bible says that a husband should love his wife even as Christ loves the church (Ephesians 5:25). This means that he is to love her to death. Kenneth wasn't even capable of loving me for six months straight. How could I have expected him to love me for a lifetime? He wasn't capable of loving me because I was not the one for him. My persistent attitude kept me from seeing that.

I can remember thinking at times that I wouldn't really mind not being cherished as long as Kenneth was mine forever. When this thought entered my mind, I should have known that there was a major problem! Sister, do you understand that you and I deserve the best simply because Christ says we do? We certainly don't want less than what He says we ought to have.

You can learn from my mistakes—check your sense of self-worth by taking a cold, hard look at your relationship. Are you settling for less than the best? You are a jewel in Jesus' crown, and you deserve to be treated with dignity.

During those terrible times, I was experiencing a fear that many women have, and especially those in the African-American community. I was deeply afraid that I wouldn't be able to find a man better than Kenneth. He wasn't just a Christian, but a man who was growing spiritually and was fully devoted to God and ministry. He was extremely handsome and was sought after by many women. Besides, he had shared several years of my life and knew me well. I was so afraid that I would never again find a man so fine, so godly, and so wonderful as Kenneth.

There are more African-American men in jail than in college. Statistics make it clear that the odds of a well-educated, godly, attractive African-American woman finding a man of like characteristics are very slim. Statistics like this would cause any woman to think twice about turning down a brother when, "At least he's saved!"

If we truly believe that God is real and that He is omnipotent, if we honestly believe that He planned our lives before the foundation of the world, then surely statistics should not terrify us. If we are afraid to wait on God to give us the best, then we don't really believe that He'll do what He says He will do.

I mean, we talk the talk! We look spiritual and carry our big Bibles around. Everyone at our jobs knows that we are Christians —we even do some witnessing. But when push comes to shove, our lack of patience simply means that all our great talking we do is just that . . . *talk*. We don't really trust that He is able.

"LET US GO OVER TO THE OTHER SIDE"

I recently came back from a ten-day trip to Israel during which I saw the Bible come to life. I got the opportunity to sing in the Garden of Gethsemene. I visited Calvary, where Jesus died, and was involved in worship services on the Mount of Olives and at the empty tomb. It was all magnificent.

But one of the most memorable events of my trip was a boat ride that I took across the Sea of Galilee. It began at the place where Jesus said to His disciples, "Let us go over to the other side" (Mark 4:35). When the storm arose that day and the sea became tumultuous, the disciples got scared. They were impatient with Jesus because He was asleep. They said, "Lord, do You not care that we perish?"

I reflected upon this incident, and I realized that there is something very important about that question. The disciples called Jesus "Lord." Now if they'd truly believed He was Lord, would they have questioned His ability to sleep in the midst of the storm? If they truly believed He was Lord, then they would have trusted Him when He said, "Let us go over to the other side."

As I sat on the Sea of Galilee in a boat, I noticed something that will always be etched in my mind. The Sea of Galilee is not that big! You can easily see across the water to the shore on the other side. Undoubtedly, the wind and the waves made the other side look farther away and harder to reach. But it really is extremely close. When it comes to taking you from where you are into the phase of life He has chosen for you, will you trust in the Lord to take you to the other side? Your destination may be a whole lot closer than you think. You need to trust Him through patient obedience as you wait on Him. Remember, you are a jewel— a jewel on layaway.

JUMPING THROUGH HOOPS

When God made the plan for our lives, I am so glad to know that He did not check the statistics. But statistics about the availability of eligible men isn't the only thing that gets in the way of our trust. When we totally trust God, we also know that we should never accept a man who is less than what Christ says we deserve. There are only two reasons why we would do that: Either we don't believe in God's ability, or we don't believe that we deserve the best.

In my relationship with Kenneth, I downplayed my own beauty, gifts, and talent so much that I doubted that I was worthy of another great guy. Have you ever done that? Maybe you are afraid to lose the relationship you have. Maybe you're saying to yourself, "This is the best I'm going to get. He's kind, handsome, and he loves the Lord."

Yeah, I know all of that. But my question to you is, does he love you? Sister, if he's not crazy about you when you are in your element (bad hair day, baggy jeans, and a T-shirt because you're tired), and you are always trying to do certain things to "keep this relationship from falling apart," then you have two problems. You have a self-esteem problem, and you have a relationship problem.

First of all, you need to value yourself, and your man should do the same whether you are dressed for the prom or for an old-fashioned day at the park. Second, please remember that if you are jumping through small hoops now to keep him happy, you will be jumping through much bigger hoops once you are married. And the more hoops we're willing to jump through, the less we really treasure ourselves just the way we are.

There was no dating recorded in the Bible, at least not the American form of dating. A godly man saw whom he wanted and he went after her. When a man pursued a woman, he did so with one thing in mind: marriage. He did it because he was ready to settle down with a life partner.

The Bible says to "guard your heart" (Proverbs 4:23 NIV). It is extremely important that we protect ourselves against the kind of men who pursue us without godly motives. One of the most destructive things you can do is to hang onto a man who is not the one the Lord has for you. When the relationship ends, that man will take a part of you with him, and more than likely he'll take a huge portion of your self-esteem as well.

As I mentioned in chapter one, Elisabeth Elliot is one of my favorite authors, an excellent teacher on the subject of dating and relationships. She describes how we should relate to men in the rather startling words of her mother: "Always keep men at arm's length!" There is only one man whom you will spend your entire life with—at least that's your hope and prayer. This means that all of the other men you are dating or have dated are not only a waste of time, but they are stealing something from the man to whom you will make your ultimate commitment. And many times the theft comes through hurt, disappointment, loss, or a deeply broken heart. You won't trust the right man because another man did you wrong.

How many times will you allow your heart to be broken and re-mended before you just decide to let God do the choosing for you? It isn't necessary to date a lot of men before you make up your mind which one you would like to marry. God will make it clear to you. But the amount of clarity that you can have about God's choice for you will depend upon the amount of baggage that you have with you. Many of us carry around tons of emotional baggage and then wonder why we cannot attract a stable man.

We have been hurt so many times and our self-esteem has been so stripped away that we wouldn't know the right man if he rode up to us on a white horse, dressed in shining armor, and with an angel sitting on his shoulder to announce that this, indeed, is the man of God's choosing! We've become so untrusting and so afraid from all of the past hurt that we simply cannot discern God's will.

I am not going to tell you how to date or whether to date, but this I will say: God's Word tells the unmarried woman to rejoice in her singleness. The Lord promises in Isaiah 54:5, "Your Maker is your husband—the Lord Almighty is his name." Have you given God the opportunity to love you? Maybe some time spent alone with Him is exactly what you need to restore your self-esteem.

And if God is your husband then you certainly don't need to be dating someone else, do you? To date anybody else would mean devoting time and attention to someone besides God. If you wouldn't consider doing that to your earthly husband, then why would you do it to your spiritual Husband?

To save yourself all of the hurt that you might carry with you into marriage, maybe some time alone with God is not such a bad idea after all. Sometimes we date so that various men can carry us emotionally until "the right one" arrives. God wants to carry you emotionally until then. That way there will be no emotional baggage. There will be no self-esteem issues. There will be no broken hearts.

PURSUED OR PURSUING?

Once you've spent time with God, and you think He may have shown you the man He has in mind for you, what comes next? How can we make certain that we get the man that we want, the way we want him, and when we want him? *Cosmopolitan* tells us to be forceful and direct. *Essence* magazine says that women need to make the first move and not play games. *Vogue* suggests that you should make yourself very available and wear the kind of seductive fashions that promise to attract a man.

These suggestions may be popular. But they are wrong and are tricks of the devil. We are never, and I mean *never*, to throw ourselves at a man. It doesn't matter what our intentions may be, whether we hope to develop a romantic relationship with him or only a friendship. There is no reason to accidentally call a man. There's no reason to voluntarily introduce ourselves to him, or to impulsively give him a business card. He can get all the information he needs if he wants it.

Isn't it amazing the amount of time we spend planning those little accidental meetings with the guys we like? There is no need for you to leave a note of encouragement in a man's box. There is no need to wear his favorite color every other day, or to make sure that you just happen to be in the cafeteria when he is. Don't go to the registrar's office to request his class schedule so you can just happen to be in one of his classes next semester. Don't loiter around his car or drive around his house.

If you are anything like me, then at one time or another you've probably made every effort to wear the right thing or to be in the right place at the right time. By the end of the day you are a wreck and probably saddened by the fact that the guy didn't notice you anyway. Sister, just rest! The Bible says to "be still, and know that I am God" (Psalm 46:10 NIV). Another translation speaks directly to us: "Cease to strive and see the salvation of the Lord." Wow! We can cease to strive and work and plan and scheme; we can just sit back and let God take care of the rest. What a relief!

Can you believe that God already has this husband thing worked out? He is already preparing your husband for you. This means that you can rest easy, knowing that God's plan is the best plan for you. In fact, our efforts to make things happen prove that we don't really trust God the way that we say we do. This became apparent to me when I pressed so hard to develop a relationship with Kenneth. I was worn out both physically and emotionally. During that time I would often pray to the Lord and tell Him that I trusted Him wholeheartedly. Those prayers sounded really good. Too bad they were lies!

The fact is, God really does know how to put the right people together. And godly men who are looking for a lifetime partner aren't interested in women who are chasing them around twenty-four hours a day. A godly man wants to find a woman who lives a quiet life while waiting on God. He is looking for a wife with a "gentle and quiet spirit" (1 Peter 3: 4).

Several of my male friends have ended relationships with women they loved. The women literally scared them off by being too desperate, too impatient, and too pushy. One man told me that he was going to surprise his girlfriend with a ring and a proposal. At the time, his eyes glimmered with the anticipation of spending the rest of his life with the woman he loved. However, that glimmer slowly faded as the woman became anxious and demanding. They eventually broke up.

One young lady I know picked out her wedding dress. She started one list of people she wanted to invite to the wedding and another list of people for the bridal party. Whenever she tried to talk about these plans with her boyfriend, he would say, "Why don't we wait until the appropriate time to discuss that?" This would make her very upset. She thought any old time was appropriate, since they had been discussing marriage for so long. Surely the big day was rapidly approaching!

This constant pressure on the woman's part caused her boyfriend to lose interest in her, and eventually he ended his relationship with her. Why? She had simply been excited about her new life with him. She had only wanted to make their wedding beautiful. Why was he being so insensitive? The reason was obvious. She had moved into his role as initiator and planner. She had usurped his God-given authority.

Any time a woman illegitimately usurps the leadership of the relationship, you can be sure that chaos will ensue. I can promise you that. I not only know because of what I have seen, but because of what I have done. My own mistakes in my relationship with Kenneth illustrate this point all too well. I am absolutely certain that one reason our relationship didn't work out had to do with my aggressiveness. This caused him to recoil and move away from me.

Satan wants you to take the lead in this area of your life. He knows that he can keep you from total happiness with a man if you continue to take the lead. Do you remember the Garden of

Eden? That was his approach with Eve. Satan didn't approach Adam in the Garden; He approached Eve. He went to the woman with one thing in mind. He wanted her to take the leadership role in her relationship with the man. When she did so, all hell broke loose.

WOMEN OF MATCHLESS WORTH

You say, OK Priscilla, that's real interesting. But I'm reading this book to learn about my self-esteem. What in the world does initiating a relationship with a man have to do with that? Sister, it has everything to do with your self-esteem. The woman who is always pursuing a man doesn't think she's good enough for him to pursue her. The woman who takes the lead, determined to get a man by any means necessary, doesn't believe that a man will ever come after her and seek her love. She thinks she has to work extra hard because she's really not all that beautiful, lovable, or desirable, and no one will notice her unless she relies on her various schemes. This woman doesn't believe that the all-powerful, all-knowing God has given her both the external and internal beauty necessary to attract the right man's attention.

A man needs to feel like he has accomplished something. A woman's job is to be still and trust in the Lord. This doesn't mean sitting still and doing nothing. It means keeping yourself occupied, doing what the Lord has called you to do right now.

Consider Ruth. In the Old Testament, we read that Ruth was busy doing what she felt God had instructed her to do—taking care of her mother-in-law with all diligence. Ruth had found her ministry and was dedicated to it, even if that meant leaving all her past relationships behind and possibly never marrying again. How willing are you to do what God tells you to do?

It was during this time of obedience, diligence, and service that Ruth met her husband. Boaz was her chosen man and she met him while serving the Lord. She did not seek out his attention on her own. She simply did what the Lord told her to do, and there he was. In fact, Boaz was interested before Ruth was interested in him. He questioned several people about her, and their response was to comment about how diligent she was in her service to her mother-in-law. If a prospective husband asks about you, what will people tell him? Once Boaz received a good report about this beautiful woman, he made known to her his intentions.

What if Ruth had done things her own way and made up her mind never to leave Moab? What if she had been stubborn and determined that she would not serve her mother-in-law? She had better things to do, you know. She wasn't an old woman. She could have stayed behind and dated other guys. She could have stayed behind and kicked it with her friends. She could have stayed behind and done the same old things she had been doing for years in her hometown, where she was comfortable and stable. But, oh my, she would have missed out on a new appointing and a new anointing.

Ruth had suffered the death of her first husband. She may have thought that she would never meet an incredible guy like him again. Ruth may have had doubts and she may have had fears. But she was a woman of excellence in the King's court. She was a woman of matchless worth. She entrusted herself to Naomi's God, and learned to submit to Him, to her mother-in-law, and, eventually, to Boaz.

In response, God was able to bring about a miracle in Ruth's life. If Ruth hadn't followed God's leading, she would have missed out on a new ministry and a new service for the Lord. She might have married again, but she would have missed out on meeting her kinsman redeemer. She would have missed out on the blessing of being the great-grandmother of King David and part of the messianic genealogy. She would have gained herself but lost her miracle.

God wants to bring about a miracle in your life, too. He is ready, willing, and able to take you over to the other side of the relationship issue. Do you trust Him? Are you willing to be still and see the salvation of the Lord?

Consider This

What was wrong with the way Kenneth related to Priscilla?

What was wrong with the way Priscilla related to Kenneth?

What tendencies do you have in the way you relate to men/your husband?

Do you truly trust God to take you to the other side of singleness, or do you act as if you have to do this alone?

What relationships in your life need to be given to God?

What do you expect from men whom you choose to date?

Do you want to date at all? Why or why not?

Prayer of Dedication

God, I sometimes have a tendency to take things into my own hands. I confess to You that I often want to initiate relationships and do things in my own power. I ask that You would forgive me and change me. I ask that until You deem that the time is right for me to marry that You would protect and guard my heart from someone who might do me harm. I ask that, starting today, You will begin to prepare me for the position of a wife by making me a woman of character and integrity. I need to learn to be submissive, and I need to learn how to follow my future husband's lead. I pray that You would help me to do better by causing me to follow You with all diligence and perseverance. Please guard my heart and mind, Lord. I don't want to carry around emotional baggage and scars. I don't want to have any regrets, and I don't want to have any issues that will affect my relationship with the man You will send to me. Thank You.

In Jesus' name,
Amen

_____

Today's Date

Chapter Seven

MIRACLE ON A MOUNTAINTOP

$\mathcal{A}$ princess in the King's court can expect to receive the royal treatment from her heavenly Father. As a daughter of the King, as a joint heir with Christ, she can be sure that nothing is too good for her. When she receives something from the Lord, it will be better than anything she would think to ask for, because He knows her so well and has resources she can't even imagine. If there's any rule of thumb a King's daughter should live by, it is this: Never settle for less than your Father's best for you. But here's another important point: Don't be surprised if He gives you His best gift wrapped in a package you weren't expecting.

A friend recently e mailed me this story. A young man was getting ready to graduate from college. For many months he had admired a beautiful sports car in a dealer's showroom, and knowing his father could well afford it, he told him that was all he wanted. As graduation day approached, the young man watched for signs that his father had purchased the car. He couldn't wait to receive his gift.

Finally, on the graduation morning, his father called him into his private study. He told his son how proud he was to have such a fine boy and how much he loved him. He handed his son a beautifully wrapped gift box. Curious, but somewhat disappointed, the young man opened the box and found a lovely, leatherbound Bible, with his name embossed on the cover in gold.

Angrily, he raised his voice to his father and said, "With all your money you gave me a Bible?" He stormed out of the house, leaving the Bible behind.

Many years passed and the young man became very successful in business. He had a beautiful home and wonderful family. He heard that his father had grown very old and frail, and he thought perhaps he should go to him. They had not met since that long-ago graduation day.

Before he could make arrangements, the businessman received a telegram informing him that his father had passed away and that he had willed all of his possessions to his son. He needed to come home immediately and take care of the final arrangements and the estate.

When the old man's son walked into his father's house, sadness and regret suddenly filled his heart. He began to search through his father's important papers and there he found the Bible, just as he had left it years ago. With tears in his eyes, he opened the Bible and began to turn the pages. His father had carefully underlined a verse, Matthew 7:11: "If ye then, being evil, know how to give good gifts unto your children, how much more shall your Father which is in heaven give good things to them that ask him?" (KJV).

As he read those words, a car key dropped from the back of the Bible. It had a tag with the dealer's name on it—the same dealer who had displayed the sports car he had so desperately wanted. On the tag was the date of his graduation and the words . . . *Paid in Full.*

How many times do we miss our heavenly Father's blessings because they are not packaged quite the way we expected them to be?

The boy's father gave him more than he asked for. In a similar sense, I am certain that sometimes when we pray for what we want and don't get it, it is because God has better things in store. That is why the Holy Spirit intercedes for us when we can't find the right words for our prayers (Romans 8:26). He knows what to say and how to say it.

We are often willing to accept the first thing that comes along to satisfy our seemingly urgent desire to have anybody, anything, anytime, anyplace in our lives. We often sacrifice best things on the altar of things that are permissible. For example, I get so frustrated when I see a young woman who has settled for second best in a relationship. It is obvious to you and me and everybody else that the guy she's with is not the right man for her, yet she just doesn't seem to get it. He is not what she needs spiritually or emotionally or even physically, but she is willing to settle for him.

We settle for second best not only in relationships, but also in other areas of our lives. We settle for a less-than-inspiring job. We settle for foolish friends. We settle for an inadequate education. We settle for loose morals, lazy habits, and lax financial values. It breaks God's heart to see His daughters striving for things that will ultimately destroy them. It hurts me because I have been there, and I know firsthand how hard it can be to let go of our desires and give them to God.

NICKELS AND DIMES

I have the most gorgeous little niece in the world. Kariss is seven years old now, and I happen to think that she is perfect, just as any aunt would. When she was about four, she had an infatuation with nickels. She was always on a hunt for as many nickels as she could find, and she would often ask family members for them.

One day she asked me for one. At the time, all I could find was a dime. I reached out to give her the dime and she let out a sob, "Aunt Silla, this is not a nickel! I want a nickel!"

I tried my best to explain to her that the dime was worth twice as much as a nickel. I told her that even though it looked smaller and less expensive, it actually had a higher value.

Kariss looked at the dime very closely and then threw it to the ground. She was determined to have a nickel. She cried and begged me for something that was not worth as much as what I'd offered her, unable to understand that she was asking for something of less value.

How many times have you cried and fought for a nickel when God wanted to give you a dime?

As we've already seen, most women long for a wonderful relationship with a man. As we wait for God to send the best to us, it is important that we remember a couple of key things when we meet a young, single man who looks like a possible mate. For a moment, set aside those things that would normally help you to make a decision concerning a man, and consider what the Lord has said in His word. There are two terms in Scripture that define what your mate should be for you and to you. These things will separate the nickels from the dimes. If you are already married, pray that the Lord will continue to develop these characteristics in your mate.

First, your husband should be a *savior.* Of course, he cannot take the place of your heavenly Savior, the Lord Jesus Christ. But just as Christ sees you, so should your husband. Just as Christ loves you unendingly and unconditionally, so should the man in your life. His love should not simply be understood, but it should be announced through his words, his actions, and his passion toward you. "For the husband is the head of the wife, as Christ also is the head of the church, He Himself being the Savior of the body" (Ephesians 5:23).

We women can be hard on ourselves. We aren't perfect, and we know it very well. We've made some bad decisions, and sometimes our history almost destroys us through guilt. However, this guy in your life should see you as a pure woman of God just as the Lord Jesus Christ does. He should not hold your sins against you and make you feel as if you are any less sensational because of a few past mistakes. He should see a beautiful, royal princess when he looks at you, because that's exactly what you are.

WASHED WITH PURE WATER

Once I was introduced by telephone to a young man who really wanted to be in a relationship with me. We talked over the phone for several months, and during those months I continued to tell him that I was not interested in a serious dating relationship. Not only was I turned off by the fact that we were separated by distance, but I was also still under the influence of Kenneth. I explained more than once that I didn't have anything to offer him emotionally. I told him that we could be friends and no more.

Well, this guy didn't take no for an answer. He was very persistent. After about six months of conversation, I had to go to Chicago. He asked me if I would mind if we met for the first time in Chicago. He wanted to drive up and see me. "That's fine," I told him. I figured after six months of phone calls, it would be nice to finally meet him.

When I got to Chicago, this gentleman did many wonderful things for me. I couldn't accept many of the gifts he tried to give to me because I knew the relationship would not go beyond a friendship. However, there was one gift that I just could not refuse.

First of all, he had the hotel staff fill my room with roses. I thought that it was gorgeous as I entered, but one thing I noticed was a pitcher with a white towel over it. There was also a bowl on the floor nearby. I couldn't figure out what it was. I asked him, and when he explained it to me I thought I had just died and gone to heaven.

He said, "Priscilla, for the last six months you have been telling me that you do not have anything to give me emotionally. You have been telling me that you are drained and are not ready for a relationship. Well, if you feel like you don't have anything to give that means that you think somebody has taken it away. I want you to know that you are holy and pure. Will you allow me to wash your feet to symbolize that purity?"

I couldn't believe what I was hearing! No one had ever washed my feet before. This guy didn't know anything about the heartache that I was going through with Kenneth—I'd never told him. But God used him to minister to me in an unforgettable way.

That evening I consulted with a godly friend over the phone. He suggested that I allow this young man to wash my feet since he was ministering to me, but to make sure he understood that this did not mean we were moving on to another level in our relationship. I agreed.

Before he did anything else, the gentleman read Proverbs 31 to me. Then he got down on his hands and knees and washed my feet, all the while reminding me of my purity before the Lord.

"Priscilla," he said, "I don't know about your past and I don't know what has gone on in your life emotionally. Actually, I don't care, but this I do know. You are a beautiful woman whom the Lord loves and in whose eyes you stand pure."

I cried as the cleansing water washed over my feet, for with it came the cleansing power of the Holy Spirit over my life. Although we never entered into a relationship beyond friendship, this man ministered to me in a way that no other man ever had. We remain good friends to this day. His demonstration of how a husband should relate to a woman he wants to marry is indelibly sketched in my mind. He will know what it means to be his wife's savior.

"BECAUSE HE FIRST LOVED US"

Just as the Lord loves us in spite of ourselves, so should our potential husband. Ephesians 5:25 says that husbands ought to love their wives just as Christ loves the church. How does Christ love the church? He loves her unendingly, passionately, enough to lay down His life for her.

Is your significant other laying down his life and taking up his cross to be with you? Does he even consider doing little things to make you happy? Do things always have to be done his way? Now don't take advantage of what I am saying. I am not suggesting that everything you want should be done your way. We certainly need to be matched to a man who is a leader and who has the power to tell us no when we need to hear it. However, there is something refreshing about a man who is willing to do things for us that are not necessarily the most convenient thing for him, just because he loves us.

There is one more thing I must point out about Christ our Savior. Why do we love Christ? Simple—because He first loved us (1 John 4:19). That is what makes His love so beautiful. He loved us when we didn't care a thing about Him. He loved us and pursued us when we couldn't have cared less about Him or His plan for our lives. In fact, He loved us so much that "while we were yet sinners, Christ died for us" (Romans 5:8). Please remember that this is how much your husband should love you. This will make him your savior.

A surprising number of married women will tell you that when they met their husband they wouldn't give him the time of day. They weren't even thinking about him. It didn't matter to them whether he lived or died. Yet despite (or maybe because of it) the fact that the woman was not initially interested in the man, he pursued her more and more until he loved her into loving him back. This is precisely the way that Christ woos us. He loves us when we aren't remotely interested in Him. He loves us anyway and pursues us continually until we finally love him back.

Listen closely to this because I don't want you to miss it: I truly believe that one of the greatest tricks of the devil is to get you to deny the love of a man who truly has the love of Christ for you because you think that you can do better. Right now, you can probably think of some guy that has been on your trail for quite some time and you haven't given him a second glance. He has pursued you and pursued you and has not given up. In fact, the more he tries the more turned off you are. You are passing up the dime because you are more attracted to nickels.

Several times I have not been interested in a guy whom, for some reason, my mother saw as a good catch. She would look at me and say, with a little smirk on her face, "Priscilla, you'd better learn to love that man!"

Although I never took her advice about those particular guys, I understand her point. Sometimes we are so in love with the butterfly feelings that we forget to look for more serious things— qualities that really matter. We are often so concerned with the package that we don't care what's inside. Of course if the man who has been pursuing you is not a Christian or isn't living for the Lord, then I am not talking about him. I am referring to that godly man whom you are skipping over because he is too short or too tall or not fine enough or rich enough for you. I am talking about those little silly reasons that Satan has planted in your head to keep you from receiving the best possible mate for you.

The biblical story of Hosea outlines for us the power of a loving husband. God commanded the prophet Hosea to take a harlot for a wife. God did this because He wanted to make a point to His people about how much He loved and cared for them.

Hosea took this unholy wife and loved her as only a savior could. Even when she had relationships with other men, Hosea went and found her, brought her home, and loved her more. He loved her because he was compelled by a greater force to be a part of her life. He wanted her even when she failed him, because the call of God was on his life to love and adore this woman. I don't know about you, but I want a husband who believes he has been called to love me and adore me as only a savior can.

SPIRITUAL ROLE MODEL

No matter how spiritually your man talks or how godly he seems to be, every day you should see an attempt on his part to make you more like Christ. Ephesians 5:26 says it this way; "He might sanctify her, having cleansed her by the washing of water with the word."

Does the man in your life know the Word? How is he supposed to sanctify you with the Word if he isn't familiar with it? Not only must he know God's Word, but he must also be able to understand it. Simply put, this man must be your spiritual leader. He must lead by example through his life and his attentiveness to God and His Word.

Far too many women compromise in this area of their lives. They see all kinds of great qualities in a man, but one notable exception—his spiritual life. I am not suggesting that he needs to be a pastor or a theology professor or a Bible scholar, but I am suggesting that he should be intentionally growing in his spiritual life and seeking to understand Scripture. That way he will be better equipped to lead you and your family into a closer relationship to Jesus Christ.

Unfortunately, for most of us, our history is marred by various things that we are ashamed of and afraid to admit. Our self-esteem is damaged and we don't feel good about what we have to present to our husband. I have great news for those of you who feel this way. God has provided yet another means through which you can realize His grace extended to you. And your husband is the tool He uses.

Men are very powerful creatures in the lives of women. They basically define who and what we are and how we see ourselves. At the very beginning, God gave Adam the job of naming every creature. In biblical days, the names that were given to all creatures meant something. Well, Adam named the female "Woman," and with that name he gave her an identity.

Today men still give us our identity. They name us by the way they treat us. If they treat us as if we are guilty, that is certainly how we will feel. Have you ever noticed that a man in your life can make you feel pretty or fat, funny or boring? You feel the way he sees you. This is simply because God has given men the power to rename or redefine women. And we want to be married to a man who gives us a good name. Whatever we do, let's make sure we choose a man who sees us through the eyes of Christ.

Maybe there is a guy who has pursued you for quite some time and you haven't looked his direction because he doesn't give you goose bumps on your arms and butterflies in your stomach. I suggest you take a second look. Those feelings are not necessarily going to happen with a man who will be your savior and sanctifier. In fact, goose bumps can be pretty deceiving, and may even be the work of the deceiver. Don't be fooled by pursuing your heart. Rather, pursue God and His righteousness and "all these things shall be added unto you"(Luke 12:31 KJV)—including the butterflies!

FAITH, OBEDIENCE, AND SACRIFICE

Genesis 22 tells the story of Abraham and the test the Lord put him through. According to Scripture, Abraham was one of the godliest people who ever lived. He was willing to do whatever it took to please God. Sometimes God puts us through the fire in order to test our love and devotion to Him. So God told Abraham to take Isaac, his son of promise whom he loved dearly, and to offer him up to the Lord.

135

Wow! Now that is serious. The Lord told Abraham to take his only son and to sacrifice him on an altar.

The next verse tells us that Abraham rose early to fulfill the instructions that the Lord had given him. Now I am sure that he wasn't the least bit excited about doing what the Lord had told him to do. He certainly was not jumping up early because he couldn't wait to sacrifice his son.

This process was undoubtedly one of great pain and suffering. He was dreading what the Lord was asking him to do. He rose early to fulfill the plan of the Lord. No lollygagging when it came to the Lord's work—Abraham did what the Lord commanded, and he did it with expedience.

He went to the mountain that the Lord had specified and told his servants to wait at the foot of the mountain. He said to them, "Stay here . . . and I and the lad will go yonder; and we will worship and return to you" (v. 5).

"Now, that is contradictory, Abraham," his servants must have muttered to themselves. "How are you going to go and worship the way the Lord says for you to worship, and still return with your son? God has asked you to worship Him by offering Isaac up. Killing him! How can you say that you will both return? You must know something that we don't, because, from our point of view, you are a little confused, sir!"

Abraham wasn't confused. He trusted in the promises of God. You see, one chapter earlier, God has said to Abraham that "through Isaac your descendants shall be named." The Lord had made a promise to Abraham that Isaac would be the door to the future for Abraham. Since that promise had already been made, Abraham could rest assured that God had something up His sleeve.

All Abraham knew was what the Lord had promised him. Was he willing to give up the nickel for the dime that the Lord had waiting? I am sure he thought that just maybe he'd heard the Lord wrongly. Surely the Lord didn't mean his son Isaac whom he loved dearly. Certainly there was something else that the Lord meant. However, Abraham was willing to do what the Lord said to do.

MIRACLE ON A MOUNTAINTOP

How about you? What about me? Are we willing to sacrifice those things that we love for the sake of Christ Jesus? I can think of many things that I am not sure I am willing to wholly give up and devote to God. Abraham was truly a faithful man. Abraham so trusted the Lord that he not only talked about the sacrifice that he intended to make for the Lord but he was also actually willing to go through with it.

I'm a talker for a living. Four or five times a month I go off to some part of the country where I will speak to women and men. I absolutely love what I do. But I have discovered that the great challenge in what I do is to actually follow through on all the things that I suggest to others. It is really simple for me to talk a good game without following up with a good walk. I remember recently being interviewed on TBN, and one of the questions that the host asked me was what was the hardest thing for me in ministry. That answer was pretty easy. The hardest thing for me is what is called, in theological circles, the difference between orthodoxy and orthopraxy.

Orthodoxy is the central belief of the historical Christian faith. Orthopraxy, on the other hand, is the lifestyle you put into practice as a result of that theological foundation. I have a lot of difficulty in that because it is hard to be a woman who lives right and serves God in our day and time. I often feel like I am talking a good talk without living up to it.

Abraham didn't seem to have that problem. Although what the Lord asked him to do was very hard, he did more than talk. He "stretched out his hand, and took the knife to slay his son" (v. 10).

It was not until he was actually in the process of slaying his son and offering a sacrifice to God that "the angel of the Lord called to him from heaven" (v. 11). You see, God wanted to wait to see Abraham's true level of obedience before He sent His deliverance and blessing. He had to wait until that crucial moment between obedience and disobedience to determine whether or not Abraham was for real.

Do you really want to be a woman in the King's court, or do you just want to look like one? Are you just putting on a show?

Abraham was very serious, and his actions proved that. Are you serious? In the words of one author, "Will the real women please stand up!"

Finally, just at the last moment, Abraham's deliverance came. Just when he thought that it was over, that all the promises God had made to him in the past were no longer valid, God stepped in and once again saved the day. The angel said to him, "Do not stretch out your hand against the lad, and do nothing to him; for now I know that you fear God, since you have not withheld your son, your promised son, from Me" (v. 12).

Then Abraham looked up and saw a ram in the bushes behind him. That ram had probably been there all the time, but he saw it only when the Lord allowed him to—only when it was time for the deliverance of God. Abraham was shown the victory of God because he was willing to be obedient and to follow the instructions that the Lord had given him.

Remember how God gave Abraham specific instructions as to which mountain he was to go to in order to sacrifice his son? Well, what if Abraham had decided to go to another mountain instead? What if he had not gone immediately when the Lord told him to? That ram might not have been there. Abraham might have missed his deliverance.

Abraham's deliverance came through his total obedience to God. His obedience led him to a place where a miracle was waiting in the strangest place imaginable—at the top of the mountain of sacrifice. Will you be totally obedient to God? Will you sacrifice all the things that you love dearly so that finally God can send you the ram, the deliverance, the victory?

God wants to do so much more than just grant our desires. He wants to give us what we *need*. To simply provide what we want would be much too easy for our heavenly Father. Singles today have dating services and technical matchmaking programs that can easily do that. We live in a day and time when getting hooked up with somebody has been made effortless. All we have to do is call into our favorite radio station and register with their "soul mate" line, and we will soon be connected with the person of our dreams. We can settle for any old job or any type of friends.

Well, God is not interested in that. He does not want to be your Great Expectations counselor. He is not interested in sending you just any old thing that you think is good for you. He wants you to sacrifice the things that you hold most dear so that He can show you Himself in a brand-new way.

God wants to give you a miracle.

THE GIFT OF A LIFETIME

A couple of months before my relationship with Kenneth ended, I got a call from Hilton Hotels asking me to come and speak at one of their awards luncheons. The event was to take place in March of the following year. All of the directors of Hilton's national reservations offices would attend this quarterly meeting.

Anita, the woman who booked this event, had picked my name off of a list of a hundred potential speakers. I gratefully accepted the invitation. A short while after the arrangements had been made, Anita called to tell me that she had been showing my information around the office in order to let everyone know who would be speaking at their next luncheon. She'd handed out a flyer with my biographical information and my picture on it, and when one of the men in the office had received it, he had begun to laugh.

"What's so funny?" Anita asked him. She assumed that he was someone I had dated before.

He corrected her theory quickly and said, "This is my pastor's daughter."

Anita then proceeded to call me and tell me about this wonderful Christian guy who was so absolutely fabulous. According to her, all of the women in the office liked him because he was so kind and gentle. She couldn't wait for us to meet in March.

As for me, I couldn't have cared less. I was still consumed with Kenneth and wasn't interested in meeting anybody new. Besides, I knew very well that if a guy is as wonderful as the one Anita described, he is bound to be terribly unattractive. And I didn't know Anita from Adam. Why should I listen to her?

Since the event was still about four months away, I went on with my life and soon both Anita and the conversation were eclipsed by other events. In December Kenneth and I finally called it quits and I really relinquished control of the situation to God. I finally gave my future to the Lord and told Him that I would let go and do whatever He had called me to do—with or without Kenneth.

Exactly three months later I went to speak at the Hilton luncheon. I had totally forgotten about Anita's offer to have me meet this guy about whom she'd spoken so highly—that is, until he walked through the front door. I caught him in my peripheral vision and decided to take a closer look. This man was so fine, so handsome! Right about then I remembered that Anita had wanted to introduce me to someone. Could this be the man she'd told me about?

Sure enough, Anita introduced me to Mr. Jerry Shirer. We talked briefly, and he told me that he knew who I was because he'd been going to our church for over five years. Since we have four thousand people in the congregation, and Jerry usually sat in the balcony, we'd never met.

Our conversation that day, March 9, was a short one. Jerry didn't ask for my phone number. On my way home, however, I checked my home voice mail from the car. Jerry had already tracked my number down and left a message asking me out to dinner. I returned the call, and two days later we went on our first date.

This man was everything I had ever wanted. All of the things I had prayed, wished, and hoped that Kenneth would do, this man did without a second thought. He was more than I could have ever hoped for. Because of my past hurts, my fears, and my emotional baggage, I gave him a hard time, but he was persistent. Even when I said that I wasn't interested in a committed relationship, he was committed to me.

Jerry went to talk to my father without my knowledge to ask permission to date me. He was determined, and I liked that. One day after we'd dated about six months, he said that he wanted to take me to the mall. We went to a nearby shopping center and he began to take me into jewelry stores to look at engagement rings. I almost died. I couldn't believe he was that serious. How could he be so sure about me after such a short period of time?

The trip to the mall happened on a Thursday. That Sunday

my grandmother pulled me aside and said, "Priscilla, you know that I don't ever interfere with your personal life, but I just have to say that you should get Kenneth out of your mind. And pay closer attention to this new guy that's hanging around. Every time I see Jerry, he is just looking at you like he will love you and cherish you and adore you for the rest of your life. He has so much love in his heart for you. You should marry him!"

You know, when your grandmother says stuff like that, you feel like the Lord is speaking directly to you! I couldn't believe what I was hearing. She had no idea that he had taken me to see rings just three days before.

Well, I called Jerry and told him that we could move toward marriage and see what happened. But I was still scared. "If I can't decide in six months," I cautioned, "then we definitely need to go our separate ways."

As days turned into weeks, it became more and more obvious that this man was all that I had prayed for. Other guys had been nice to me before and had treated me in wonderful ways. But they had all come at the wrong time. This man came after my sacrifice to the Lord. After I was willing to let go and let God take control of my love life, this man was my ram. He appeared after the sacrifice was made. And if I hadn't made the sacrifice, I would have missed my deliverance, my miracle, my victory.

On November 26, 1998, Thanksgiving Day, Jerry asked my father if he could marry me. Being the type of father he is, my dad waited until December 26 to tell Jerry to put his request in writing! (My grandfather had made my father do the same thing.) Jerry wrote my father a beautiful letter explaining to him why he loved me and why he wanted to marry me. Two weeks later my dad wrote Jerry back and gave him permission to ask me to marry him.

On February 12, 1999, Jerry proposed to me on live television in Dallas. As I was doing some interviewing on one of our live television shows, Jerry stepped up and popped the question on the air! There was a violinist, roses, everything. It was a beautiful memory that I will have forever—on videotape. Jerry Shirer is all I have ever wanted in a husband. We were married on July 24, 1999, in Dallas.

Consider This

If you could paint the perfect picture of how God would send you a mate, the scenario would go like this . . .

If you are already married, how does this compare with the way you and your husband got together?

Do you truly believe that God can do things for you that go beyond your wildest imagination?

What does God want you to sacrifice for Him?

What is the hardest thing for you to sacrifice to God? Why?

How will you know when your miracle has arrived? What are you looking for in a mate? A job? Friends?

Are you willing to wait on God's best? Explain.

Prayer of Dedication

I worship You, Lord, because you are the God of miracles. I thank You that when I think all hope is gone, You still have another plan of action in mind. I praise You, Father, that when what I want isn't the best for me, You have something better. I celebrate the fact that according to Your Scripture You can do more than I can ask or think. I do have thoughts about what I want my _____ to be like, but I trust You. In fact, I trust You not just in this area but I make a commitment to trust You in every area of my life. Whether I am searching for the perfect job, house, or mate, I will trust that when things look like there is no hope and no answer, You are still in control and You have a ram waiting in the bush. Thank You that You can still perform miracles. I look forward to the miracles that You are about to perform in my life!

In Jesus' name,
Amen

_____

Today's Date

RESETTING THE STONE

By now you've heard a lot about being a jewel in the King's crown. But you still may be discouraged. Perhaps in your head you are beginning to believe that the Lord thinks you are precious and priceless, but you can't quite get it into your heart. If that's the case, you need to give God the opportunity to reset the unique and beautiful gem of your life, so you can know for sure that you are a sparkling addition to His crown.

It could be that you've been in a relationship in which you were stripped of your self-respect. You so desperately wanted someone's approval that you sacrificed yourself on the altar of their acceptance. Maybe a relationship with a friend or boyfriend has come to an end and you feel like a failure. You might have been abused as a child, or you have abused yourself with negative self-talk about your appearance or capabilities. Possibly emotional, mental, or physical illness has taken its toll on you. Whatever your particular circumstances are, the God who loves us is able to lift our spirits and remind us of our significance.

GOD'S LAW OF GRACE

I learned many things in seminary—some things about God and some things about myself. I can remember sitting in one class, holding a tissue in one hand (just in case the tears started to pour—I was still hurting over Kenneth) and taking notes with the other. Dr. Lanier Burns taught that particular class, and I was so moved by his words. He started to talk about the theological term *creational worldview.* As I took notes, I had no idea that what he was about to say would change my life.

The creational worldview goes something like this: If God can make the grass grow and if He can cause the skies to bring forth rain; if He can keep the earth spinning on its axis at a distance neither too near nor too far from the sun to keep humans alive; if He can illuminate the entire earth with the light of the sun, stars, and moon; if He could conceive an atonement plan for the salvation of the entire world, surely He can take good care of you and me.

If almighty God can manage the universe, then He's got you covered. At some point in your life, you have probably felt very defeated, convinced that nothing could remove you from the pit you were in. Let me introduce you to Jesus, the author and finisher of our faith!

Jesus has promised that He will be faithful to complete the good work He began in you the moment you became a woman in the King's court. You are His rare jewel, and He is determined to refine you into the most brilliant gemstone possible. He thinks that you are worth the effort, and He hasn't forgotten who you are. Have you?

Your family might be keeping its distance from you because you got pregnant before marriage or because you just can't seem to kick the habit of drugs or alcohol. You look at yourself in the mirror and feel so inadequate. Your dead-end, eight-to-five desk job makes you feel claustrophobic. You have always wanted to be your own boss and set your own hours, but the plans for your new business never got off the ground. Well, rest assured: What God thinks of you supercedes what the world thinks of you and what you think of yourself. God's opinion outweighs yours and everybody else's. Isn't that good news?

As I sat on a plane recently, it dawned on me that the aircraft was defying the law of gravity. Everybody knows that what goes up must come down, yet we weren't falling from the sky. Why? The law of aerodynamics that we were utilizing as we flew superceded the law of gravity. Well, hallelujah! That's what Christ's blood does for you and me. It overcomes the law of sin and death.

In human terms we may deserve very little respect and honor, but as women of the King's court, we benefit from a new law that supercedes the old. God's Word says, "You were dead in your trespasses and sins" (Ephesians 2:1). But this is not the case anymore. We've been freed because of the new law, "For sin shall not be master over you, for you are not under law, but under grace" (Romans 6:14).

Sin masters us and keeps us bound and unfulfilled. Ironically, the very things that we thought would bring us fulfillment and joy are the things that steal our peace and our power. It's possible that your sins—even the ones you just think of as bad habits—are keeping you from reaching your potential in Christ Jesus. But don't despair! I want to remind you that you no longer have to be bound. According to my favorite Scripture verse, Galatians 5:1, "It was for freedom that Christ set us free."

Jesus wants you to be free to shine for Him in a way that you never thought possible. He has provided the means, and that means is called grace. The new law of grace supercedes the old laws that have kept us from reaching our full potential as royal women. And that new law can bless us with new radiance and beauty.

THE MORE YOU'RE FORGIVEN, THE MORE YOU'LL LOVE

Jesus paid special attention to those who needed Him most. He was interested in hanging out not with the Pharisees, but rather with those who were afflicted with disease and spiritual darkness.

The Pharisees thought that they knew everything. They wanted to impress everybody around them with their fancy clothes and fancy knowledge. They thought they were far too righteous to need help from Jesus. In fact, they wanted to make Him look as bad as possible because He was distracting others from them and their piety. You know what? They got exactly what they wanted— nothing at all! If you don't know you need help and aren't willing to get real with God, then you won't get anything from Him.

But you and I know that we need Him, and we've decided to get real with Him. Now let's take Jesus up on His offer to love us unconditionally, to love us right out of the pit that we've dug for ourselves. He says, "It is not those who are healthy who need a physician, but those who are sick; I did not come to call the righteous, but sinners" (Mark 2:17).

There was a woman who came to Jesus one day. She was a sinner, and the whole town knew it. She was broken, inside and out. She felt utterly destroyed and had no clue anymore about her beauty and value. She was saddened by her history of sin and her hidden actions, and she'd almost given up hope.

Jesus was eating dinner with a group of Pharisees that day. This woman boldly walked into the dining room and found a place for herself at His feet. She sat there and cried, allowing her hot tears to drip on Jesus' feet. Then, to the amazement of everyone there, she began to wipe the feet of Jesus with her long hair. No one could believe how daring this sinful woman was, wiping the feet of Jesus with her hair.

The Pharisees had been trying everything in their power to entrap this man. They wanted to expose Him as a fraud, and up until this point they had not been able to do it. They couldn't get any evidence against Him. But now here He was, sitting with a woman of ill repute and allowing her to touch him. She was a filthy woman who had disgraced herself for years.

The Pharisees took careful note that Jesus did not even flinch when she sat down beside Him. He had nothing but compassion in His eyes for this woman, this sinner. They asked Him how in the world He could justify sitting with a woman like that and allowing her to touch Him in such an intimate way. I mean, they wouldn't have sat with her. They would have immediately had her escorted out of their presence.

When they questioned Jesus, He simply said that she who is

forgiven much will love much (Luke 7:47). That was the end of it. No rebuke, no judgment, no bad treatment. Jesus simply forgave her.

Maybe you have willfully entered into an unholy relationship and now you are suffering for it. Or maybe your lack of self-worth is because of another's sin. Whatever the case may be, the Lord is standing next to you with outstretched arms, inviting you back to Himself, back to peace and joy and back to the realization of your true value and worth in Christ Jesus. Just come now and sit—sit at the feet of Jesus. He will smile sweetly, wipe your tears, and forgive your sins.

REBUILDING THE TEMPLE

The book of Haggai is one of my favorite books in the Bible. It's quietly tucked away in a few pages of the Old Testament, but its message is a powerful one. The Bible does not tell us much about the prophet Haggai. We don't know about his background or lineage, but we learn from this book that he had a heart for people to realize their potential in the Lord. He had the solution for the problem described in the book of Haggai, and He has a solution for you and me as we struggle to rebuild our lives.

During Haggai's time, the Babylonian army had completely wiped out the city of Jerusalem, including the temple. Now you must understand that the temple was the central rallying point for all the Jews. The crowning glory of the city was the temple. It was a jewel that the people of Jerusalem were proud to call their own.

The activities of the nation of Israel centered around the temple, giving the people not only a sense of unity, but also a place to meet with God. For generations the temple had been a source of joy and pride. Now it was gone. Not only was the temple gone, but also the Babylonian army had taken the Jews into captivity so that they couldn't even attempt to rebuild the temple.

What has Satan taken from you? What "temple" has he taken from you in an attempt to steal your pride and joy? Maybe your virginity is gone. You gave it away even without a fight, and now you desperately regret it. Maybe your self-respect is gone. Maybe you've lost your husband or your family.

Or perhaps you feel that you're being held captive by Satan.

You feel like he has not only stolen your temple, but has also taken you into captivity so you can't even attempt to rebuild the center of your life. He has shaken you so deeply, so severely that you feel like a gem that has become loose in its setting. You need to be reset.

After several years the Jews were released and allowed to return to their homes, and their first priority was the rebuilding of the temple. However, several enemies did their best to keep the temple torn down and out of commission. Those enemies knew that if the temple were rebuilt, the Jews would regain the spiritual, political, and military power they had lost. They would once again pose a threat to other nations.

So Israel's enemies did their best to keep the power point of this community down. (Do you have any friends like that?) However, after some time passed, it was no longer their enemies that were keeping the Jews from building the temple. The Jews themselves had become strangely satisfied with living without the center for worship. They stopped their rebuilding efforts. Spiritual paralysis had set in.

Perhaps they were just sick and tired of trying. Their hard work had seemingly gone unnoticed by God. They were weary of all the opposition. Whatever the reason, they became complacent and satisfied with the fact that they didn't have the temple any longer.

Have you become complacent without your temple? Have you lost something very important, and instead of trying to get yourself straightened out, have you become spiritually paralyzed? Maybe you were once interested in trying to rebuild your temple, but all of the lazy friends you hang around with have rubbed off on you. Now you no longer have the willpower necessary to get the job done.

GETTING THE GLOW BACK

When I was young, my dad and mom used to always take us to the circus, and we kids would always want Daddy to buy us the little glow-in-the-dark thingamajigs. You know, those colorful gadgets that you tie around your arms, legs, and neck and they just glow. We thoroughly enjoyed them. But not long after we got home, we would be disappointed because the glow would be gone. My parents were particularly upset after spending all that money!

Then my dad discovered a little trick. If he wrapped those little things around a light bulb for a while, they would glow again. And after they were removed from the light bulb, their glow would be gone again within a few hours. We had never noticed before that when they are displayed, those colorful toys are always sitting underneath a source of light. That's where they get their glow.

Well, maybe your glow is gone just like Israel's glow was gone. Maybe you have lost your fire and illumination. It probably has a lot to do with the fact that you are not hanging around the light. You need the light of the Word of God and the light of friends who are going to encourage you and set you ablaze with their desire to live for Christ. If your glow is gone, check out who and what you're wrapped up in.

Although the Jewish people gave up on their attempt to rebuild the temple, God wasn't satisfied with their decision. So he raised up the prophet Haggai and gave him the job of telling the people what God thought about their little pity party.

The Lord spoke through Haggai and the very first thing Haggai did was to tell the people to look inward. He told them to look at themselves and the mess they'd made trying to do things their own way and in their own power. God says in Haggai 1:5–7:

Consider your ways! You have sown much, but harvest little; you eat, but there is not enough to be satisfied; you drink, but there is not enough to become drunk; you put on clothing, but no one is warm enough; and he who earns, earns wages to put into a purse with holes. . . . Consider your ways!

The people had used every excuse in the book for not rebuilding the temple. They said that the time had not yet come (1:2). But Haggai revealed their laziness for what it really was—just a lame excuse. The people didn't have time for the Lord's house but they'd certainly found time to build their own houses—paneled houses at that (1:4). Their priorities were not straight. They had time for everything except what the Lord had commissioned them to do. And they were reaping the consequences.

Meanwhile, God's people were trying to fill themselves up on food and drink and money, but they still were not being satisfied. You know why? You can do anything you want, but if it is not what God has called you to do, you will be unfulfilled and unsatisfied.

Today God wants you to "consider your ways." What are you doing that is keeping you from reaching your full potential as a woman of the King's court? What are you doing that is keeping the gem of your life from being securely set in the crown of the King? Could it be your fault that you need to be reset and resecured?

Every attempt you make to fulfill yourself in ways God has not designed for you will not only leave you unsatisfied but will also ultimately keep you from reaching your full potential. Maybe you don't think you are doing anything wrong with your time and energies. You aren't sinning, but what about the encumbrances that are keeping your temple unrestored? Anything that is not aggressively involved in your temple's rebuilding is what Paul calls, in the book of Hebrews, a "hindrance." We don't have time for hindrances.

TIME AND SAND

Even the bad things in your life can be used by the Lord to teach you some invaluable lessons that couldn't be learned otherwise. When the Babylonians destroyed the temple, the Jews were experiencing hardship and couldn't figure out why. God could have stepped in at any time and made them do His work. But in His wisdom the Lord wanted them to learn some great lessons that they would not have learned if He'd stepped in too soon.

One of my favorite professors at Dallas Seminary was Dr. Ronald Allen. He is an awesome teacher and friend. He was one of my favorite professors because his class was always fun and exciting. One evening during a class that I took with Dr. Allen, he interrupted his train of thought to tell us something that seemed unrelated to the discussion at hand. He just felt the need to share it with us, and it was really powerful.

Dr. Allen said, "You know, class, the desert has sand and God has time."

We all looked at him in bewilderment. We had no idea where he was going. But this is what he told us. The children of Israel were in the desert for a very long time. They had been freed from captivity and were now in the wilderness, waiting for God to bring them to the promised land.

They had been waiting a long time and were starting to disbelieve the promises of God. They didn't know if they could trust His words anymore, because their fulfillment was taking so long. They had seen Him work miracles in Egypt, and they knew He had brought them safely out of bondage, but now their faith was wavering.

God had fed them from the sky and had quenched their thirst from a rock. He had saved them by allowing them to walk through the Red Sea on dry land and had killed their enemies by closing up the sea on Pharaoh and his army. The Israelites had seen miracle after miracle, but they still grumbled and complained and questioned God's ability to take care of them. Because of their disobedience and unfaithfulness, God's people were made to wander in the wilderness until that generation of Israelites was dead. And now their children were wandering in the same wilderness.

God looked down and said, "Look, I have given you a promise of what I will do for you if you will simply obey. Now, you can be like your parents and wander around for another forty years. Or you can trust Me, follow My lead, and do what I have called you to do. The choice is yours. *I have as much time as the desert has sand!*"

Today, God makes that same plea to you, my sister. Are you going to keep doing it your way? Or are you going to let the Lord bring to pass the things He has promised? The Lord has a lesson for you to learn, but how long it takes you to learn it is up to you. You can wander for another forty years, or you can obey right now. He has as much time as the desert has grains of sand.

Do you feel like you are going in circles with absolutely no direction or guidance? Maybe your problem is like that of the Jews as recorded in the book of Haggai. They were so interested in doing their own thing that they forgot to follow the Lord and to be obedient to Him. Because of their disobedience and lack of faithfulness, the Lord said to them:

> You look for much, but behold, it comes to little; when you bring it home, I blow it away. Why? . . . Because of My house which lies desolate . . . Therefore, because of you the sky has withheld its dew, and the earth has withheld its produce. And I called for a drought on the land, on the mountains, on the grain, on the new wine, on the oil, on what the ground produces, on men, on cattle, and on all the labor of your hands. (1:9–11)

God's people were probably wondering where the drought and famine were coming from. They didn't understand that *they* were the problem. They were obstructing their own blessings. They were the cause of their inability to reach their full potential. It was their own fault.

Are you to blame for your destruction? How foolish to be in a mess and not to know that the mess was caused by your own negligence. It is more foolish still to know that you are the problem and to do nothing about it.

Thankfully, God's wayward people had Haggai to remind them to obey the Lord. And you, my sister, have me! I am here to remind you to obey Christ *right now*. Otherwise you will wander for another forty years. The choice is yours, but remember: God has as much time as the desert has sand.

"LORD, YOU ARE THE SAME . . ."

The Jews were busy doing their own thing and had wasted valuable time achieving the King's goals. I shudder at the amount of time I have wasted as a daughter of King Jesus. At times I have created a barrier between myself and my potential because of foolish ambitions that I thought were worth my time and effort. Many of those efforts left me with a huge void after they were finished.

Contemporary Christian artists Billy and Sarah Gaines are

good friends of mine. They gave me one of their CDs when I was fourteen years old, and this song still rings true after all of these years:

THE SAME ALL THE TIME
For I know that sometimes the things that we think are for sure
They fade like the ending of day
Sometimes the things that we think are secure
Pass away
For I know that sometimes the things that we seek and we find
Break both our hearts and our mind
But Lord, you are the same
The same all the time!

I don't know about you, but both my heart and mind have been broken and have needed mending. My sense of value and worth has been at an all-time low. This temple of mine has needed to be rebuilt. At times I have struggled to understand why certain things happened to me. Yet every situation I can think of in which I was destroyed on the inside was a situation that God had not called me to be a part of. I was building my own house with little thought about the Lord's temple, which was lying desolate. Like the people of Israel, I made excuse after excuse, and all of those excuses had left me with my own house built, but empty and un-satisfying. Only the Lord's faithfulness to me has restored me and allowed me to be reset in His crown.

BETTER THAN BEFORE

Zerubbabel, the governor of Judah during Haggai's time as prophet, was stirred with the desire to rebuild the temple. The people's spirits were rejuvenated too, and they began the task of rebuilding the house of the Lord. But then a small problem arose. The people started comparing the work they were doing with Solomon's magnificent temple, which had been destroyed sixty-six years before.

Solomon's temple had been an extraordinary piece of work, and some of the people remembered its glory very vividly. The

Jews became deeply discouraged because there was no way that they could possibly create anything as beautiful as what had once been theirs. They were disillusioned. They felt as if their efforts wouldn't amount to much in the end.

I've felt that way. Haven't you? You finally are trying to do things God's way, but it just doesn't seem worth the effort. I mean, you've already lost your virginity, so why try to be pure now? You've already done drugs and been a consumer of alcohol, so why try to clean up your act? You've already tried suicide once, twice, maybe even three times. You are already feeling defeated.

"Come on," you say to yourself. "Do you really think that it is worth all of this effort? Sure I can rebuild my temple, but why? It will be nothing in comparison to the way it was supposed to be before I messed it all up. I've done the damage now. Do you really think that this is worth my time?"

Let me tell you what the Lord said to the Jews: "Take courage . . . and work; for I am with you. . . . My Spirit is abiding in your midst; do not fear!" (Haggai 2:4–5). God has under control all of the stuff you fear. He is sovereign, and at this very minute He is working "all things together for your good" (Romans 8:28). All you have to do is trust Him and believe that He will do what He says He will do.

Why would the almighty God ask you to rebuild the temple if it could not be done and done well? Why would He want you to waste your time? Remember the creational worldview? If He can take care of the whole universe, then what makes you think that He can't take care of little old you! We serve a God who is able to do all things. It bears repeating that He "is able to do exceedingly abundantly beyond all that we ask or think" (Ephesians 3:20).

The Lord said something surprising to His people. He promised that if they continued to do what He'd asked them to do, He was not only going to give them a great temple, but He would also "fill this house with glory" (Haggai 2:7). And now, here is the good part. He makes another promise to the people, and He makes that same promise to you. Haggai chapter 2, verse 9: *"The latter glory of this house will be greater than the former"* (italics added). My sister, that's what He wants to do for you and me.

Now that is something to shout about. He wants to make us better than ever! Despite the mistakes, despite the sin, and despite the hurt and pain that has caused your low self-estimation, He wants to reset you and make you better than ever.

Have you ever noticed that the things in life that are worth getting are worth working for and waiting for? Anything that comes too easily will not be treasured, but the more effort we have to put into obtaining something, the more important it will be to us. God knows it won't be easy, but He wants you to focus on rebuilding you: your value, your worth, your potential, your self-esteem, your temple.

If you will lay aside all of the sin and encumbrances of your past and entrust the present and the future to Him, He will do more than guide you in rebuilding what has been destroyed. He will make sure your latter glory will far outshine your former glory. Isn't that amazing?

EXTRA EFFORT, EXTRA COSTS

As I write, two men are walking in and out of my apartment. They are furniture-delivery guys, and they are bringing in my new bedroom furnishings. When I purchased the furniture, I was told that delivery would cost forty-five dollars. That meant that the deliverymen would come inside, set my furniture down in its boxes, and leave.

Afterwards, I would have to put the handles on the dresser drawers and put the bed frame together. I would have to find the pliers and the screwdrivers. I would have to figure out what attaches to what, and where. I know myself well enough to know better than to let that happen. I would make such a mess that it would take my dad, husband, or somebody else hours of work to fix it. So when the delivery guys first got here I asked them a question.

"How much will it cost for you guys to do all the assembly for me?"

"Fifteen dollars," they said.

"That's not bad," I answered with a smile.

Now, in my opinion, the initial cost I'd paid for my furniture should have been quite enough to cover everything. But I was willing to pay extra for assembly, because I wanted to fully enjoy the good things I had received.

Often we feel as though life shouldn't be so tough. We are saved, and it seems to us that the initial cost of salvation, paid by the Lord, should cover all of life's repairs, replacements, and renewals. We don't see why we can't just sit back and wait for God to rebuild our temples for us. But that's not the way it works! We have to take up our cross daily and follow Him (Matthew 16:24). Doing this will cost you extra.

Just like the Jews who had to rebuild their temple, you and I have to rebuild ours. In a similar sense, although we are priceless, beautiful jewels in the King's crown, from time to time we need to be repolished and reset so we'll shine for Him with maximum beauty. It won't be easy. It won't happen without cost. But it will be well worth the effort.

Consider This

In what ways has your temple been destroyed?

What are you doing right now to participate in your own destruction?

Do you always seem to be running in circles and making no progress toward your goals? Explain.

What is the Lord asking you to do right now to begin to build the Lord's temple in your life?

Do you truly believe that God is able to rebuild the mess that you have made? Why or why not?

Why is it important for you to regain what you have lost?

Prayer of Dedication

I am committing myself to You anew today, Lord. I am broken and hurting because _____. I know that my temple has been destroyed. Today I want to begin rebuilding it.

I admit that I have been doing things my way so long that I am skeptical as to whether or not I can really rebuild my temple. But according to the book of Haggai, I am able to rebuild it through You and Your power. I look forward to seeing the final product as You work in my life. I praise you because no matter what I have done, You can now remake and reshape and remold me into a woman of greater glory.

I know that You have given me all the materials I need to build the temple. Now, Lord, give me the strength. I will give You all of the honor and glory and will proclaim Your miracles and mercies to this and every generation. I will extol You and profess You to whomever I meet. I will always say to the world that my Lord restored me and made me new. Lord, I will not fight You, nor will I rebel.

Change my life so that I am better than before!

> *In the name of Jesus*
> *and for the sake of His reputation,*
> *Amen*

> _____
> *Today's Date*

Chapter Nine

AN EMERALD CALLED GRACE

*O*f all the magnificent jewels in the King's treasure chest, there is nothing more beautiful than the emerald called "grace." In His amazing grace, God overlooks our hurts and sins and loves us just the way we are. In His grace, He looks beyond our faults and sees our needs. In His grace, this great God of ours reaches out to us every day in the most unimaginable ways. Just as we grace His crown like jewels, God's emerald of grace sparkles and shines in our lives, making us more beautiful and valuable than we could ever be without it.

DETERMINED TO MEET WITH JESUS

The book of Luke is filled with stories of how the Lord Jesus bestowed His grace on people in their most pressing times of need. When those who sought Him were desperate for His help, Jesus showed up and gave them what they needed. From the faithful disciples to the sick, from the godly to the sinful and struggling, Jesus offered His grace to people in the circumstances where they needed him most.

Christ wants to meet you at your deepest point of need, too. He wants to come alongside you and restore what has been lost. If you are like me, you need Christ to take your hand and to guide you to a place of healing. Maybe you have made a mess of your life, and your hurts and problems are too many to number. Yet it is precisely in your frailty and failure that God wants to meet with you, to challenge you to know Him more intimately and to live more successfully, to extend His grace to you.

During Jesus' earthly ministry, He touched people's lives right where they were. Consider what He did for the woman described in Luke 8.

Jesus was returning from the country of the Gerasenes, and when He got back, He found that there were many people waiting for Him. In fact, many is an understatement. There were hundreds of thousands of people. These folk welcomed Him because they had been waiting for Him. And there was one woman in this crowd that day who would have missed a life-changing experience if she had not been waiting for Jesus.

As Jesus and His followers moved slowly through the streets, a certain man approached Him and told Him that his daughter was very sick, even to the point of death. This man was an important person, an official of the synagogue, and I suspect that when he came to Jesus, everyone stepped aside to let Him through.

The people in the crowd probably realized that Jesus might not have time for all of their needs, but they must have felt fairly sure that He would have time to hear this man's request. He was important to the community, and he was a religious man. Surely Jesus would take care of Him. There was barely room enough to walk; yet this man was able to fall at Jesus' feet. Somehow space was made for Him to prostrate himself before Jesus and make His request. And this important man had a very important request to make: His twelve-year-old daughter was ill and needed Jesus to heal her.

Jesus began to make His way to this important man's house, and the crowd once again filled in and began to press against Him as He moved along. Suddenly, however, Jesus stopped in His path and looked around. He couldn't go any farther because something had caught His attention. The important man's twelve-year-old daughter was on the verge of death, yet all of a sudden Jesus was seemingly in no hurry. Instead, He stopped and said, "Who is the one who touched me?"

I can only imagine the puzzled expressions on the people's faces. I am quite sure that some of His critics must have thought that this man named Jesus really was crazy after all. Thousands of people were pressing in on Him as He walked, and yet He wanted to know who had touched Him! Even His disciples were a little concerned. They turned to Jesus and explained to Him, as if He didn't know, that there were many people around, and all of them were trying to touch Him, trying to get as close to Him as possible.

Jesus said, "Someone did touch Me, for I was aware that power had gone out of Me" (Luke 8:46).

Although many people were jostling and bumping into Jesus as He went to heal the daughter of the important man, there was one touch that He had to acknowledge. This touch actually resulted in a transference of power from Him to the individual who had touched Him. There was something unique and intimate about that touch.

Everyone looked around in bewilderment, and no one came forward, at least not right away. Then this same crowd that had made room for the important man made room for a small, delicate woman. She emerged from among the masses and fell down before the Master.

This woman had been sick for twelve long years. She had developed an issue of blood that never went away. During those times, when a woman had her period, she was banished to the outskirts of the city because she was considered unclean. There she was required to remain, excommunicated from normal life for seven days until her menstrual cycle had finished. This was obviously a very hard time for these women, as they would have to leave their friends, parents, children, husbands, and other loved ones and be sent outside the community.

How could this poor woman have known, years before, that

she was about to be sent away for good? How could she have guessed that she would not see her family and friends for the next twelve years? How devastated she must have been to find that after the seventh day, seventh month, and seventh year, she still could not return to the familiar life she had once known. She was removed from all who loved her and all whom she loved because of this endless issue of blood.

I imagine that after so much time, she had given up all hope of restoration and deliverance. Her very life was being drained from her. Everyday she was closer and closer to death, feeling the very essence of her life drip from her body. She had been tempted to despair.

She was likely frail and weak. I'm sure that the loss of blood brought with it many devastating side effects. She was dizzy and fatigued by anemia, by the lack of nourishment to the vital organs that gave her life. Her life's blood was literally flowing from her body. She could barely walk.

Then, on that special day, she heard that Jesus was passing by.

It took every ounce of her strength to get up from her fetal position and to half walk, half crawl to the street corner where she hoped Jesus would appear. She knew that she wasn't supposed to be around other people—she was unclean—but she was desperate for help. She needed Jesus. But how would she ever get to Him?

Before long, she saw Him moving down the street in her direction. But the crowd around Him was much too large, and she was much too sick to manage her way through it. Yet she was determined to receive her healing. She'd heard about this Jesus and the grace that He had for those who would accept it, so she fumbled and stumbled her way toward Him. Can you see her as she commands her frail body to stand and move forward a few feet before she crumples in a heap on the ground? She makes her way through the crowd until she is just behind Jesus.

Just as she is close enough to capture His attention, her body gives out on her again, and she falls beneath the feet of those who are trying to push past her. She can hear whispers, people speaking of her with disdain. She is tired and she is sick. She feels the tears well up in her eyes because she can't go any farther. All the strength that she can muster allows her only to reach out her skinny arm and touch the furthermost fringe of His garment.

As soon as she touches it, she collapses on the cobblestones. The tears roll down her cheeks. She's done all she can do.

I am certain that Jesus noticed this woman's touch because her faith was as strong as her body was weak. She had made so much effort to reach Him. This sick woman did not touch the hem of His garment because she wanted to. She touched it because, in her desperate attempt to get to Him, this was her best effort. She had no opportunity to explain herself to Him. All the strength that she could muster only landed her on the ground at the feet of Jesus. But it was there that she found her healing.

This woman was healed of her afflictions. She was made new because she decided to reach out to Jesus no matter what it took. She had waded through a massive, merciless crowd of people who didn't care about her or her affliction.

This poor woman had mustered every ounce of strength from her blood-depleted body to find the Master so that He could restore her to health. Her search for Jesus had not been fun. It had not been comfortable. It had not been applauded by the crowd. But it had been worth it. She had touched the hem of His garment.

How desperately do you want to meet with Jesus? Are you willing to fight with the masses? There might not be a crowd of people that we have to contend with, but there are multitudes of circumstances that keep us from falling at His feet. Our minds and lives are packed with financial worries, family concerns, deadlines, and countless other things that keep us preoccupied and unavailable to Him.

Today, my friend, Jesus is passing by. Grab hold of Him and to the promise that He has made to restore you and guide you. He wants so badly to heal you of the "issue" that has drained you of strength, damaging your life. Whether, like the sick woman, you need to bring your frail body with all its hurts and pains, or whether your "issue" is from your mind and spirit, Jesus is passing by and wants to heal you. Will you let Him?

AWAITING OUR RETURN

Our God is so powerful that all we must do is get to the hem of His garment. He loves us so much that He makes Himself available to us in any way possible. He wants us to be restored. He wants us to know about all the wonderful things He can do for us and through us. Just as the father waited for his lost son in Luke 15, so the Savior waits for us.

A father's rebellious son had left the family and taken his inheritance with him. He had decided that it was better for him to be on his own, away from the comforting arms of those who loved him. All of the great things that he had been given, he'd squandered. All of the wealth and knowledge that he had gained from His father, he'd misused and abused. Now, at last, this young boy was living what he had considered to be the good life, but discovering that he had nothing left. Not only was he doing without, but now he also found himself living with swine and eating what they ate.

The young man had lost everything.

For a while, his pride had probably kept him from going home. However, at some point he came to his senses and decided to head back to his father's house. I am sure that he returned with much humility and expected that his father would look at him in disgust and turn him away.

But what the prodigal son found was astonishing to him and to everyone around him. His father, who had been longing for his return, saw his son a long way off and ran toward him with outstretched arms. He was so excited that he presented his boy with new clothes and jewelry, and he even had a party for him.

This is a true picture of God's grace. This son was not given what he expected or deserved. Rather, he was given a second chance, a new position in his father's household. He had suspected that his father would punish him and make him a servant. Instead, his father embraced him and made him the guest of honor at a festive celebration.

God loves you so much that He not only wants you to return, but He is also *waiting* for you to return. He has so much to give you. He wants to remind you of your position as His daughter,

His princess. He wants you to remember your inheritance in Him. Even though you may have squandered some of the great gifts that He has given to you, He still loves you and wants to celebrate your return. Like the old song says, God's grace is "greater than all our sin."

AMAZING GRACE, HOW SWEET THE SOUND

The grace of God demands our full attention. It is more magnificent than anything that we can imagine, yet we take God's grace far too lightly. Without it, you and I would be helpless. No one has accomplished anything that God's grace has not allowed. Without God's grace, we can do nothing. Without it, we would perish. Grace is the very root from which we draw our nourishment to live. It is the river that quenches our thirst and the bread that provides our spiritual nourishment.

I remember sitting in conferences, conventions, and concerts when I was a young girl and seeing women of God minister in song or word. I would sit and just stare at them. So much power rang from their voice. It would amaze me that gifted women could stand before large audiences and hold their attention for long periods of time.

CeCe Winans was and is one of my favorite singers of all time. I love her voice, and I also love her style. She is always modest with her dress yet very distinguished and stylish. I even like the way that she moves her mouth when she sings.

I remember sitting and watching her for hours on end in the earlier days of her career. Any program that she was on I would tape and watch over and over again. I think deep down inside I wanted to be CeCe Winans! I am sure that there are many girls just like me who sit and watch people on stage and admire them and all they do. Speakers and singers always seem to have it all together, and it is impossible to imagine that they are hurting or struggling.

I now find myself in scenarios very similar to those that I remember as a young girl, except now I am the one who is on stage. I am the one who stands before the group and shares myself, my gifts, my testimony, and my talents with others. The Lord has given me the profound opportunity to minister to women, and it is a great privilege.

The more I speak and sing, the more I appreciate the power of God's grace. Now I know what the women I admired must have been thinking when I was watching them. I cannot tell you how many times I have stood before an audience and wanted to turn around and leave the stage because I was not adequately prepared and I knew it. It would take too long to tell you about all of the times that I had sinned miserably the week before or even the day before I had to speak or sing. Yet there I was, about to encourage my listeners to be women of the kingdom of God and to live their lives accordingly.

I have often stood before a crowd with a smile on my face and bitter tears in my heart because of something that was going on in my own life. Yet through all of that, the Lord still used me. That, my sister, is God's amazing grace. When you are in the most miserable position of your life, and it is your fault, and He still uses you, that is grace.

In fact, I have found that God works best when we are weak and He is strong. We are most useful to Him when we finally decide to decrease because "He must increase" (John 3:30). I am so glad that I serve the God of grace who uses broken people. Now when I see Christians in high-visibility positions, I look at them in a different light. I know now that it is not by some great talent or by their own capabilities that they are able to do what they do. It is because they have recognized that they need Jesus. It is because they have received so much grace, and they want to tell the world about it!

When he saw the Lord and beheld His holiness, Isaiah cried, "Woe is me, for I am ruined! Because I am a man of unclean lips, and I live among a people of unclean lips; for my eyes have seen the King, the Lord of hosts" (Isaiah 6:5).

When you encounter the King, the Lord of the universe, you realize how filthy and messed up you really are. His greatness and power reveal that you are feeble, insignificant, and weak. This is exactly where He wants us to be, for it is in weakness that His power makes us strong. Only when we realize that we cannot do anything on our own can we truly look to the heavens, just as the prophet Isaiah did, and say with meaning, "Here am I. Send me!" (Isaiah 6:8)

BY GRACE YOU ARE SAVED—AND MUCH MORE

Some people think of grace only as the path along which we are ushered into salvation. It is the means through which we obtain eternal life in the hereafter. We know that "by grace you have been saved" (Ephesians 2:8). But too often our thoughts about grace stop there. If so, we have missed out on the true splendor of our great God's limitless grace.

Of course grace is essential to our salvation. God became grace personified when He decided to reach down and extend His love and affection to us. He gave up His heavenly home and came to earth not just to live among us but also to die for us. If grace meant nothing more than that, it would still be astonishing, and we would thank God for it forever. However, God is able to do immeasurably more than all we ask or think, and even in His grace He has surpassed our imagination. Just when we think He's done all He can possibly do for us, He does a little more.

When I have Bible study with young women from a nearby university and they come to *me* to ask for advice from Scripture, I am certain that God's grace is being made evident in my life. After all that I have done wrong, He still loves me, and that is a miracle in and of itself. You and I are miracles. God continues to work though us, and that is a miracle. Why would He want to do that? He does it because He loves us.

Even after you were promiscuous in high school and college, He still loves and cares for you. Even though you had an abortion when you knew in your spirit that it was the wrong thing to do, He still looks at you with love and affection. Even though you decided to do drugs and get drunk when your Christian friends weren't looking, God still loves you. Even though you have been lukewarm and faithless in your relationship with Him, He remains faithful in His relationship with you. That is the grace of God; not just the means through which you are saved but—even more—the platform on which you are sustained.

God does not pass out His grace in prepackaged bundles to all who need it, but rather He has tailored His grace just for you. He can give you the grace to live as a single woman. He can give you the grace to live married. He can give you the grace to live your own life and take care of your aging parents. He can give you the grace to spend within next month's budget constraints for your personal or business ventures. He can give you the grace to endure the ridicule of your meticulous boss. He can give you the grace to let go of the unrealistic career aspirations you've set for yourself. He can give you the grace to get out of that fantasy world you've created that keeps you from enjoying life abundantly. He can give you the grace to be delivered from the traps set by Satan. He can give you the grace to have life and have it more abundantly!

GRACE TO GET HOME

A young woman was driving down the road, going very fast. In fact, she was speeding at one hundred miles per hour in a fifty-mile-an-hour zone. She was really in a hurry to get home from college for Christmas vacation and didn't even realize that she was traveling so fast. She didn't realize until she zoomed past a police car that was stationed on the side of the road. She held her breath as she looked in her rearview mirror, hoping that the policeman had not noticed her. Much to her chagrin, he had.

She watched as the police car pulled away from the shoulder of the road and began to follow her. She watched as the red lights flashed on. She hoped that the officer would pass her and take off after someone else, but she knew better. She pulled over.

The cop came to the window and issued her a ticket. He explained that she would have to pay two hundred dollars or spend three days in jail. She couldn't believe it! How could she miss Christmas by spending three days in jail? Problem was, she didn't have two hundred dollars.

She found herself standing before a judge. "Young lady," he said, "you have been cited for going one hundred miles an hour in a fifty-mile-an-hour zone. You can either pay two hundred dollars or spend three days in jail."

The young lady looked up at the judge with tears running

down her face; "Sir, I'm so sorry but I don't have the money. And, sir, I don't want to spend three days in jail and miss Christmas with my family."

The judge looked down at her for a moment, then explained that although he was sympathetic to her desire to be at home with her family, there were laws in that city, and they had to be enforced. Once again he declared that two hundred dollars would have to be paid or she would have to spend three nights in jail.

The young woman felt more desperate now because it seemed that the circumstances were hopeless. She started sobbing uncontrollably.

Then the judge did something that got everybody's attention. He stood up and laid down his gavel. He unzipped his robe and laid it across the back of his chair. He picked up a sport coat that was hanging on a rack on the wall and put it on. He walked down the stairs and stood next to the young girl.

The judge then reached in his pocket and pulled out a big wad of money. He counted out a certain amount, laid it on the bench, then walked back up the stairs. He took off his sport coat, hung it back on the rack, picked up his robe, and zipped it back on. He sat down, calmly picked up his gavel, hit the desk, and addressed the woman again.

"Young lady, you have been found guilty of going one hundred miles an hour in a fifty-mile-an-hour speed zone. You are guilty of breaking the law in our city, and that offense is punishable by your either paying two hundred dollars or spending three nights in jail. You claim that you don't have the money, but it looks like somebody else has paid it on your behalf. Since the fine has been paid, you may go."

The young woman stared at the judge in disbelief. "Oh, and one more thing," he added with a smile. "Have a merry Christmas with your family."

That, my sister, is grace.

When we were speeding down the road of sin and destruction, Satan pulled us over and was about to incarcerate us or make us pay a fine that we couldn't afford. God looked down, and in His unmerited favor paid the fine for us. He didn't use cash. He used His Son's blood. He offered us His only begotten Son as a means through which we could be sanctified and brought into close fellowship with Him. The fine that Jesus paid for us with His blood supercedes Satan's indictment. Grace has set us free from the law of sin and death. Will you accept His grace?

There is something else that is very important in the story I told you. The young woman made it in time for Christmas. She had a wonderful time with her family, and she was very careful to drive safely and slowly wherever she went. During the third week of her Christmas visit, she received a letter from the city in which she had received the ticket. The letter explained to her that the ticket she had gotten was not going on her record, because the amount she had paid not only covered the cost of her ticket but also provided her with deferred adjudication. This meant that extra money had been spent, over and above the cost of the fine, to eradicate the citation from her driving record.

Initially, she was a little puzzled, but then it dawned on her what had happened. Not only had the judge paid two hundred dollars to cover the cost of the ticket, he had also paid the extra amount necessary to get the ticket removed from her record so that it would not have any detrimental effect upon her.

That is exactly what Christ did when He bestowed His grace upon us. Grace is so much more than the pardoning of our sins. Grace is the extra payment that is made so that sin is no longer on our record in the sight of God. Grace means that sin no longer has any detrimental effect on our future. Jesus has paid it all. Not only has He paid for our life in the hereafter, but also His grace is covering our existence in the here and now!

Today, right now, He is extending His grace to you and to me. We are His princesses, beautiful jewels in His crown, and He wants us to grab hold of grace and let it guide us to a life of peace and rest. He wants us to realize that apart from His grace we are absolutely nothing at all. Oswald Chambers writes in *My Utmost for His Highest*:

Can that sinner be turned into a saint? Can that twisted life be put right? There is only one answer: "O Lord, Thou knowest, I don't."

Never trample in with religious common sense and say—"Oh yes, with a little more Bible reading and devotion and prayer, I see how it can be done." It is much easier to do something than to trust in God; we mistake panic for inspiration. That is why there are so few fellow workers with God and so many workers for Him. Am I quite sure that God will do what I cannot do? When God wants to show you what human nature is like apart from Himself, He has to show it to you in yourself. If the Spirit of God has given you a vision of what you are apart from the grace of God (and He only does it when His Spirit is at work), you know there is no criminal who is half so bad in actuality as you know yourself to be in possibility. My "grave" has been opened by God and "I know that in men (that is, in my flesh) dwelleth no good thing." God's Spirit continually reveals what human nature is like apart from His grace.

The closer we get to God, the more we realize how much we need Him in our lives. The more clearly we see God, the more evident His holiness becomes. The more evident His holiness becomes, the more unholy we realize we are. It is then that His grace to us becomes most apparent.

It is God's grace that makes it possible for imperfect, sin-prone women like you and me to be jewels in the crown of the Lord. We may be muddy. We may be sick and sore. We may still be battling with the sins that have caused us to fall more than once, and may yet cause us to fall again. But God isn't looking at our sin. He is looking at us—you and me—through the eyes of grace. He sees us the way He always intended us to be.

By grace, Jesus Christ has invited us into His royal court. He has offered to dress us in the finest garments. He has called us to share His glory. He has summoned us to be women of excellence. He has chosen us to be sanctified and glorified princesses—daughters of the King. What can we do but thank Him? How can we refuse His gift of grace? No matter what has happened in your life, He has given you the precious gift of today and tomorrow. The future stands before you as an open door of opportunity—the opportunity to live in the abundance that our Father gives to those who choose Him. You can choose to accept His gift or let it pass you by. It is up to you.

"And all these blessings shall come upon you and overtake you if you will obey the Lord your God" (Deuteronomy 28:2).

Consider This

How do you define grace?

In what ways has God been gracious to you?

How desperately are you seeking God? Explain.

What people, places, or things are in your way?

What "issues" do you have that Jesus needs to heal?

Do you truly believe that Christ can restore you to full emotional, physical, and spiritual health? Explain.

What steps of obedience will you take to lead you to the abundant life that He offers?

Prayer of Dedication

Lord, I need Your grace more now than I ever have before. I
have many "issues" in my life that I just can't take care of by
myself. Some of my concerns are: _____,
_____, and _____.
I know that I must seek You with all of my heart, mind, and
soul, and I am willing to do that. No matter what the cost, and
no matter what others may say, I will seek You morning, noon,
and night. I praise You because You are gracious. I am so glad
that after all I've done You still love me anyway. I can't believe
that You still want me, but, God, I praise You because You do.
Lord, I need to touch You. I need to experience You in a whole
new way. I am desirous of a relationship with You that is unlike
anything that I have ever before experienced. From this day
forth, I will seek You and with Your power I will not ever stop.
You are my God, and I thank You in advance for releasing Your
power in my life.

In Jesus' name,
Amen

_____
Today's Date